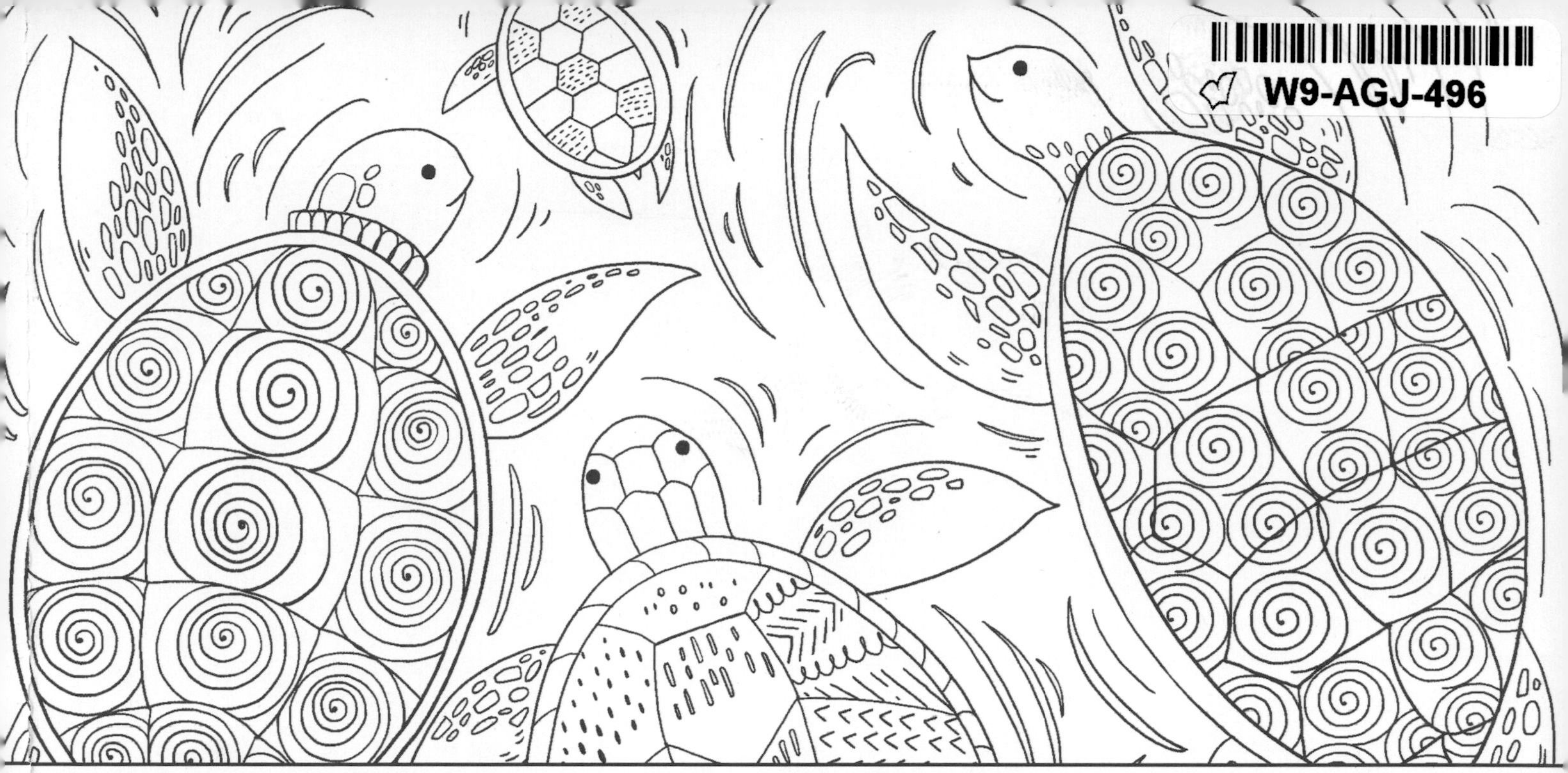

ANIMAL KINGDOM

Colour & Doodle

A collection of beautifully designed line drawn illustrations, to help colour and doodle the stress away...

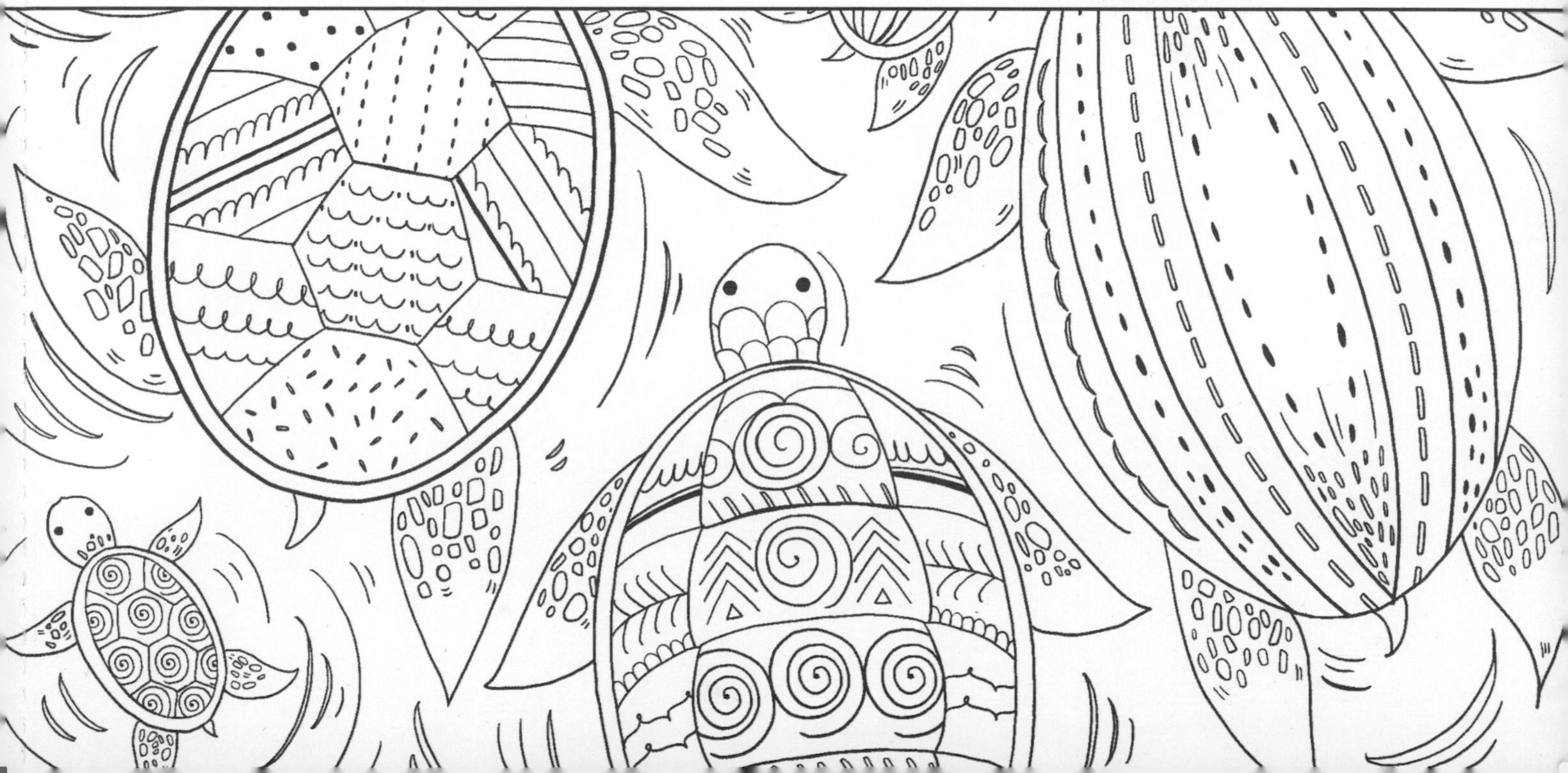

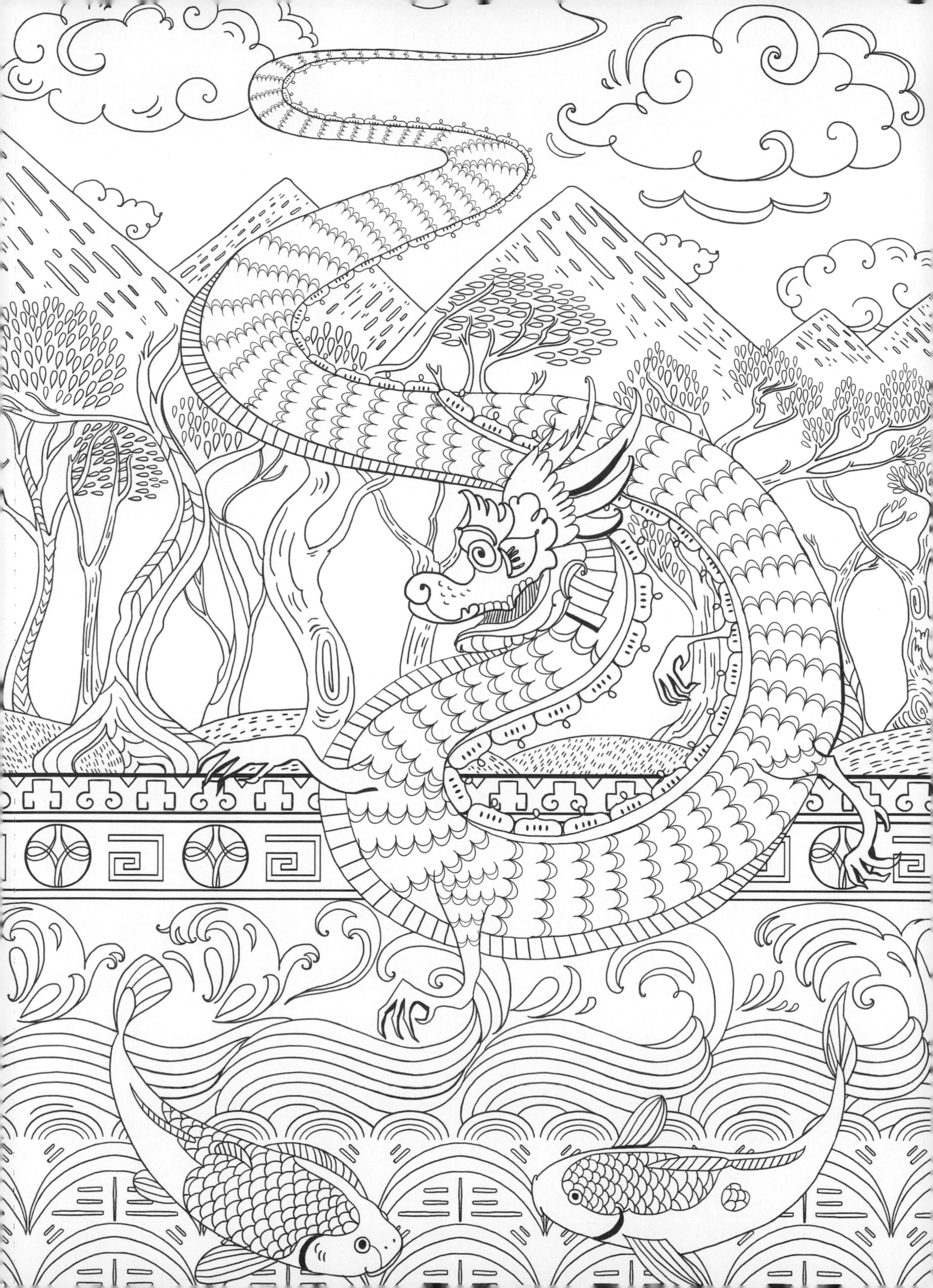

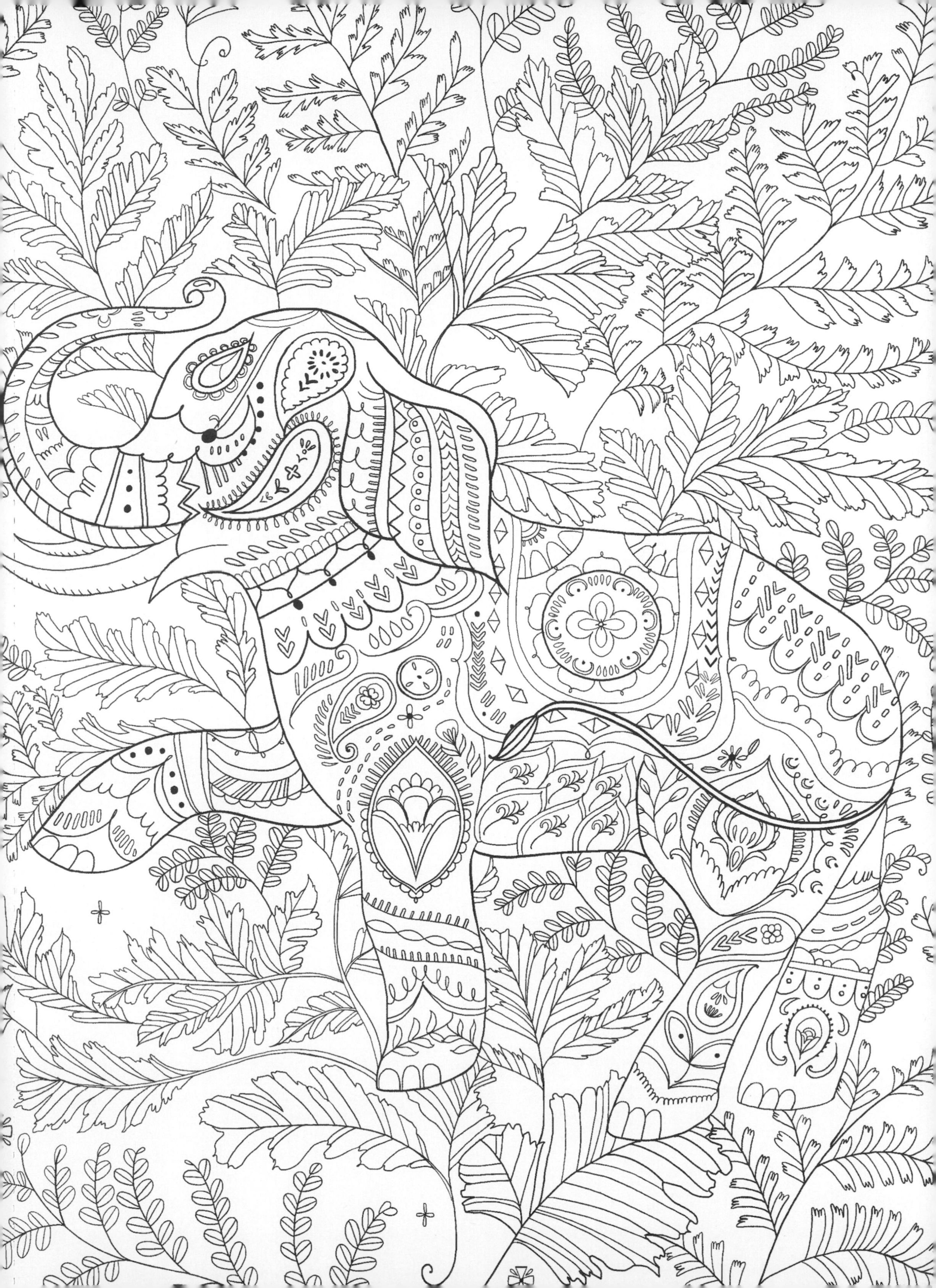

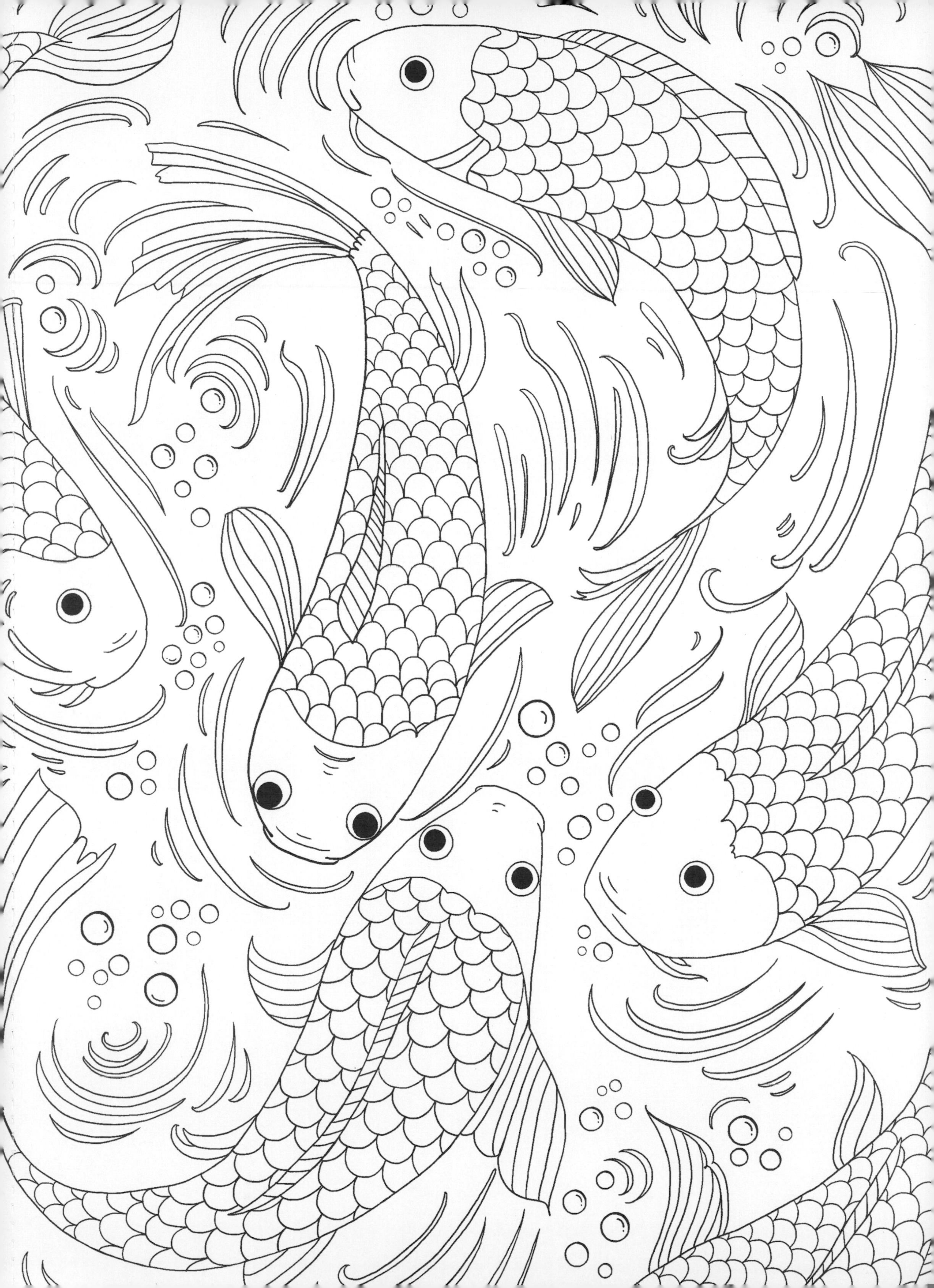

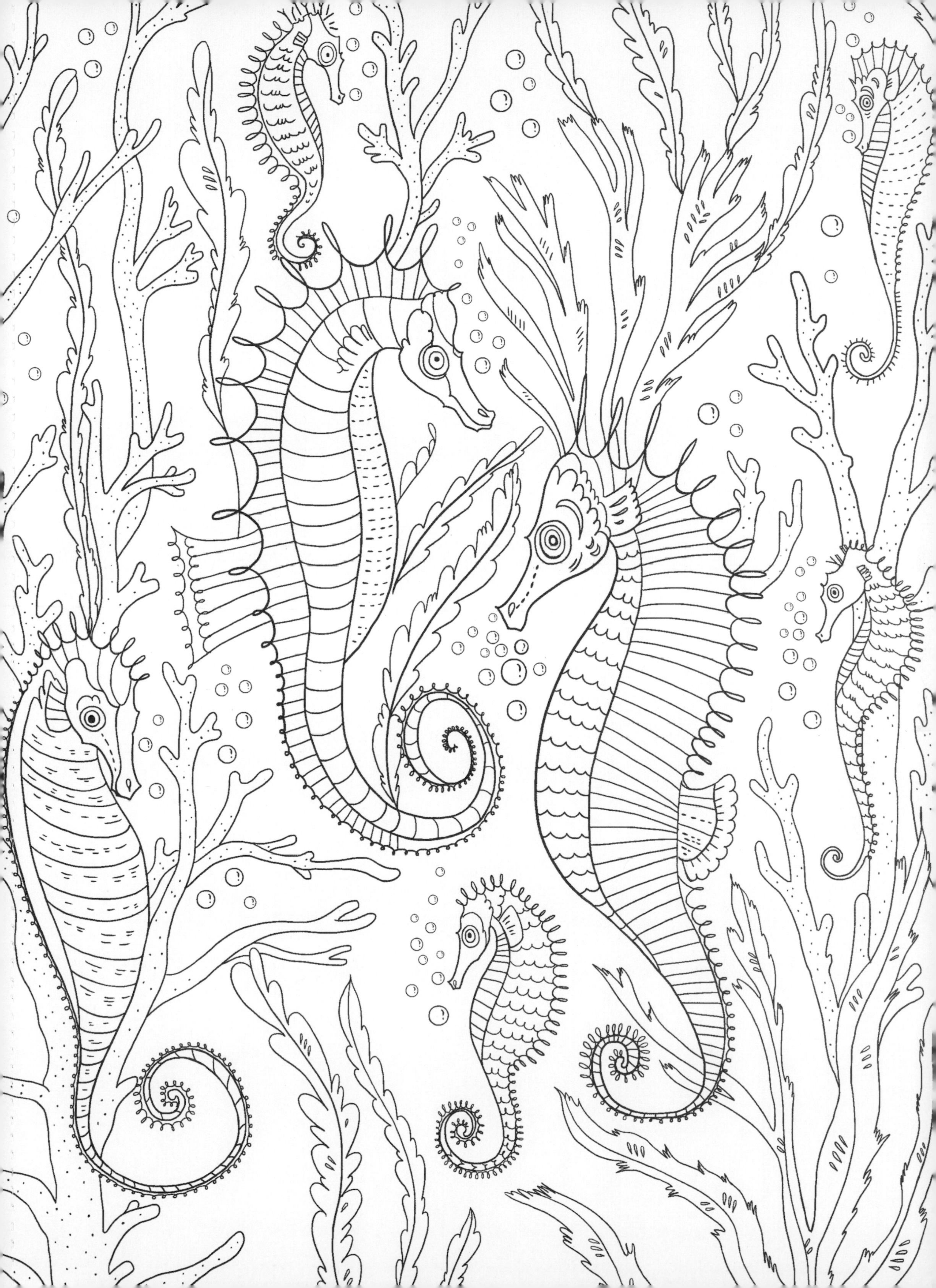

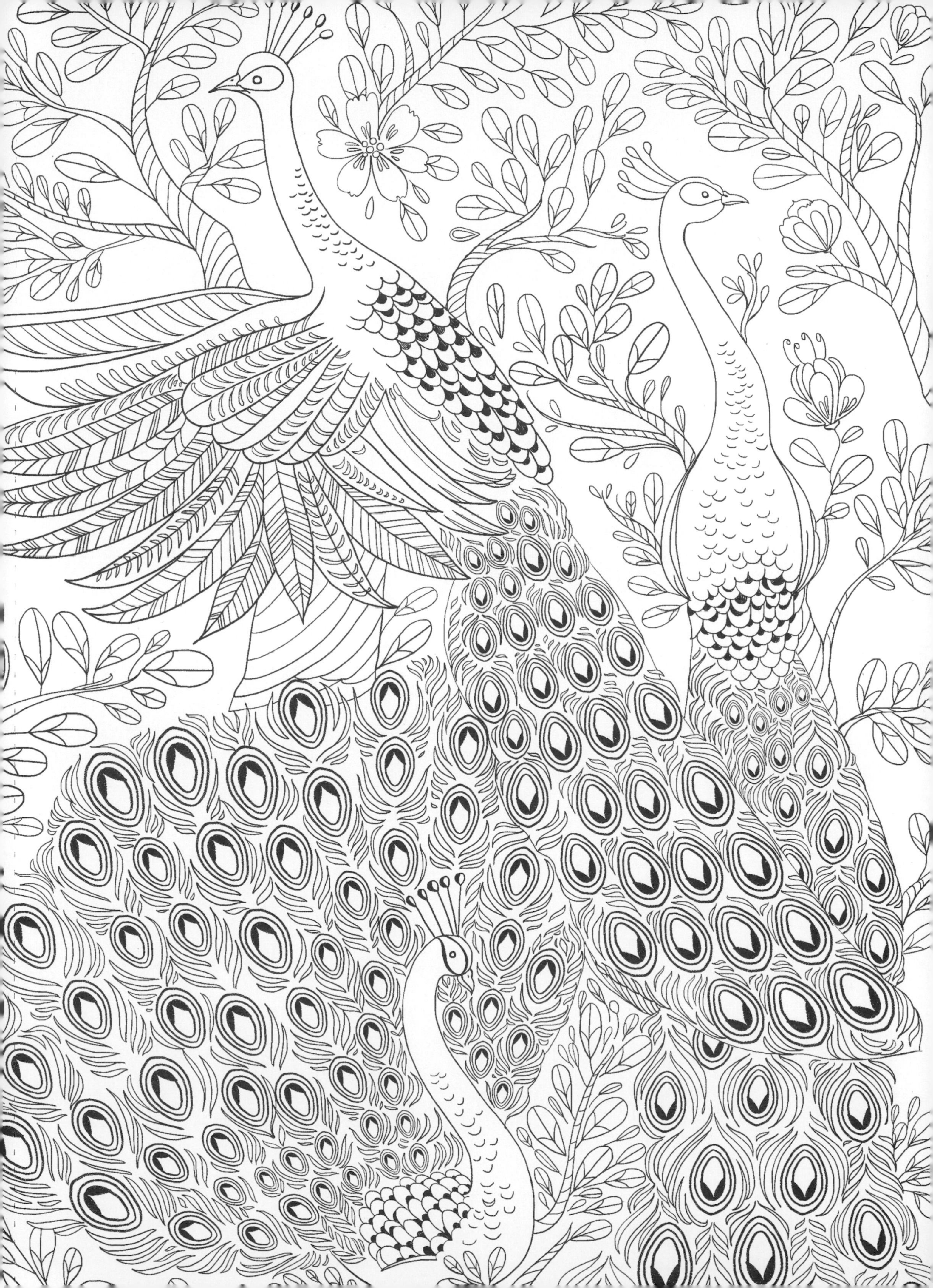

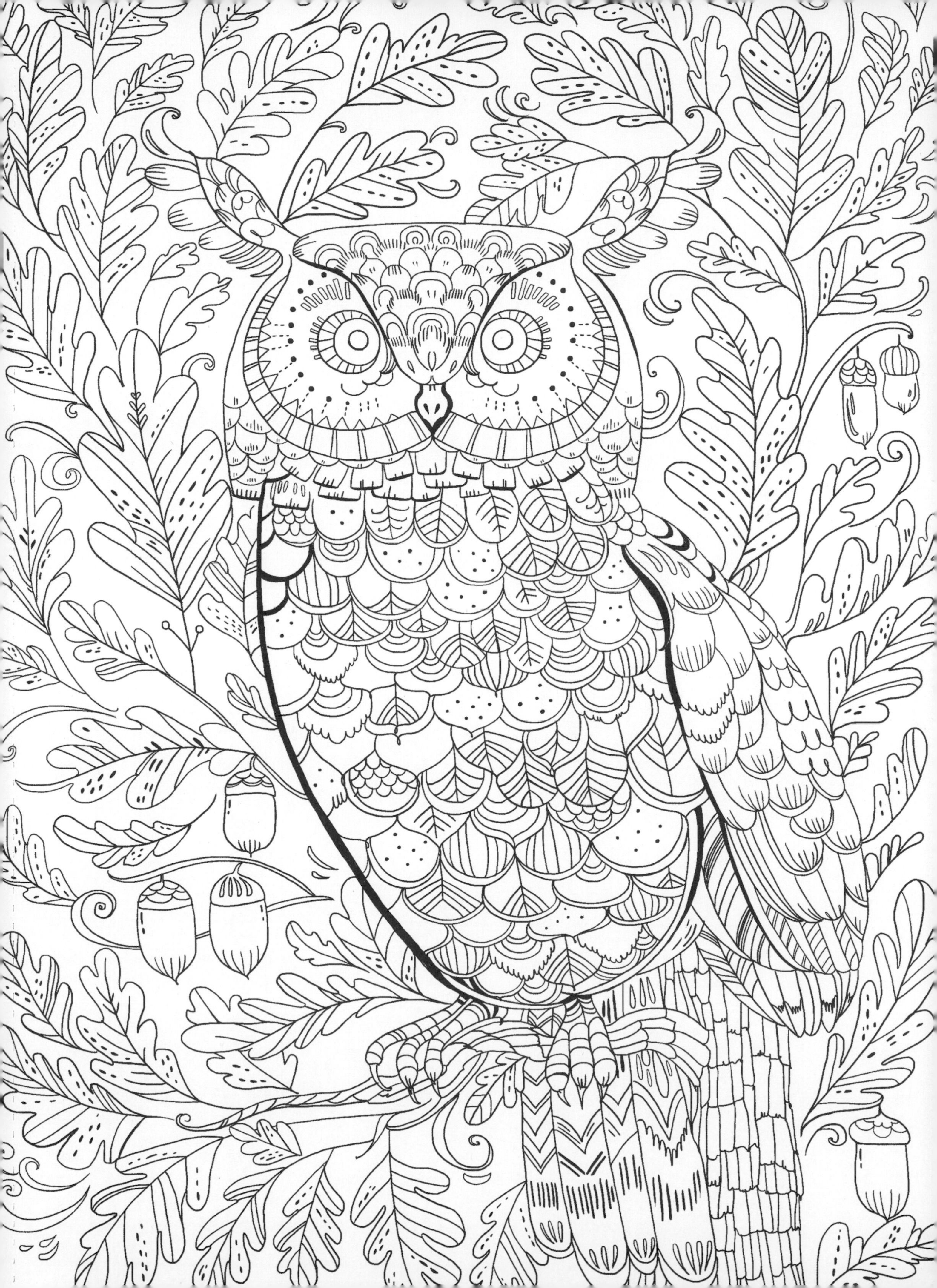

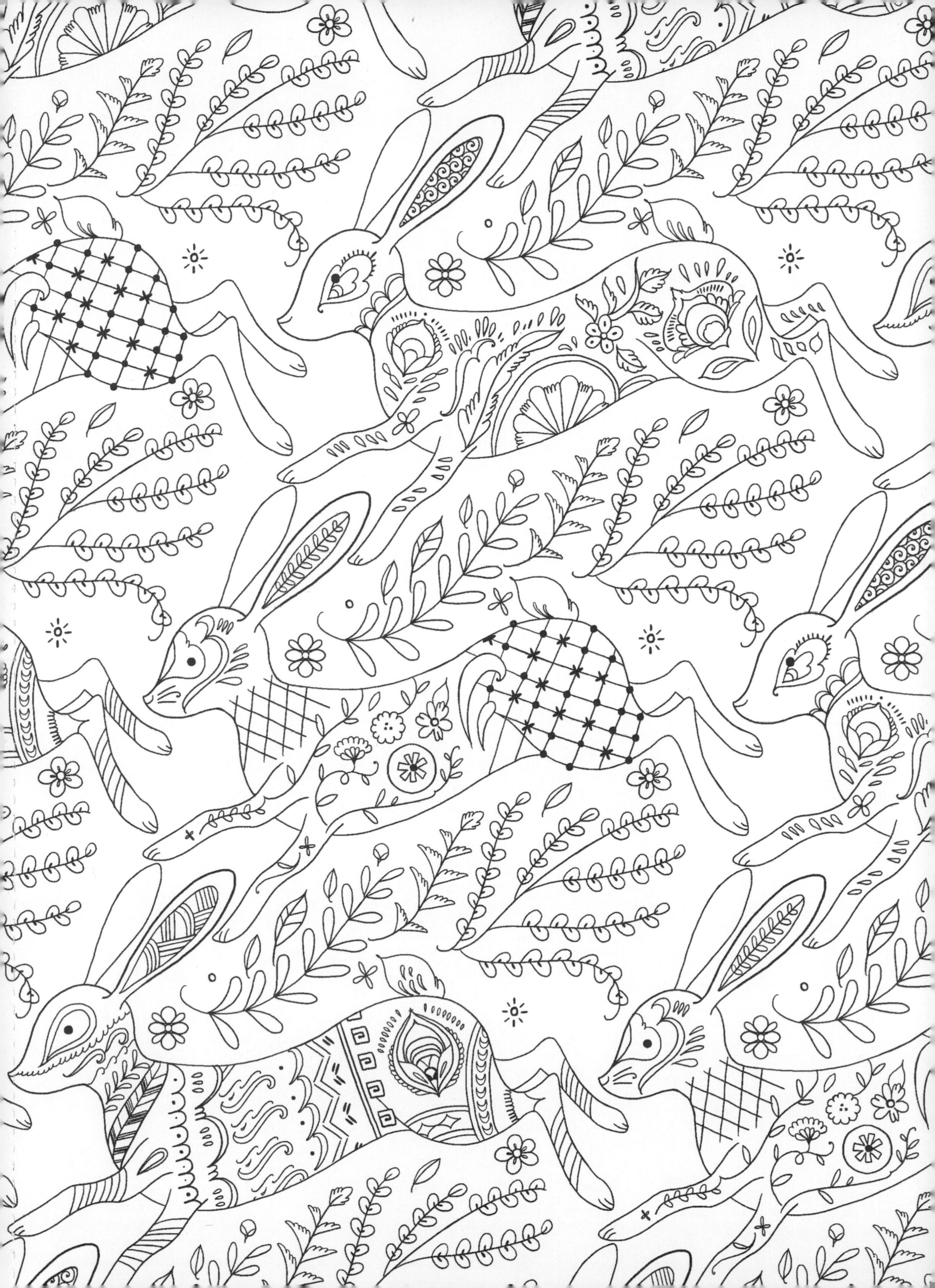

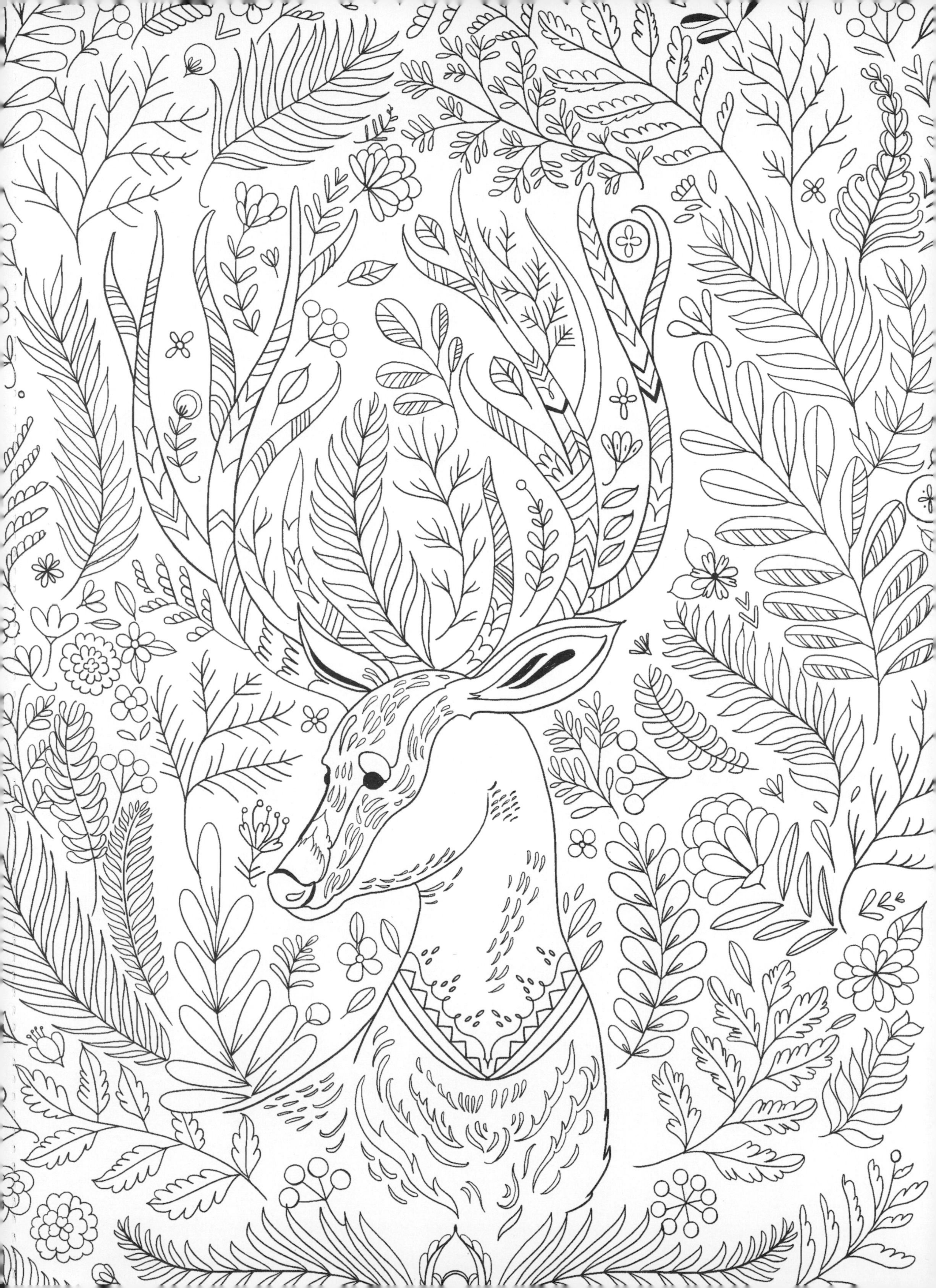

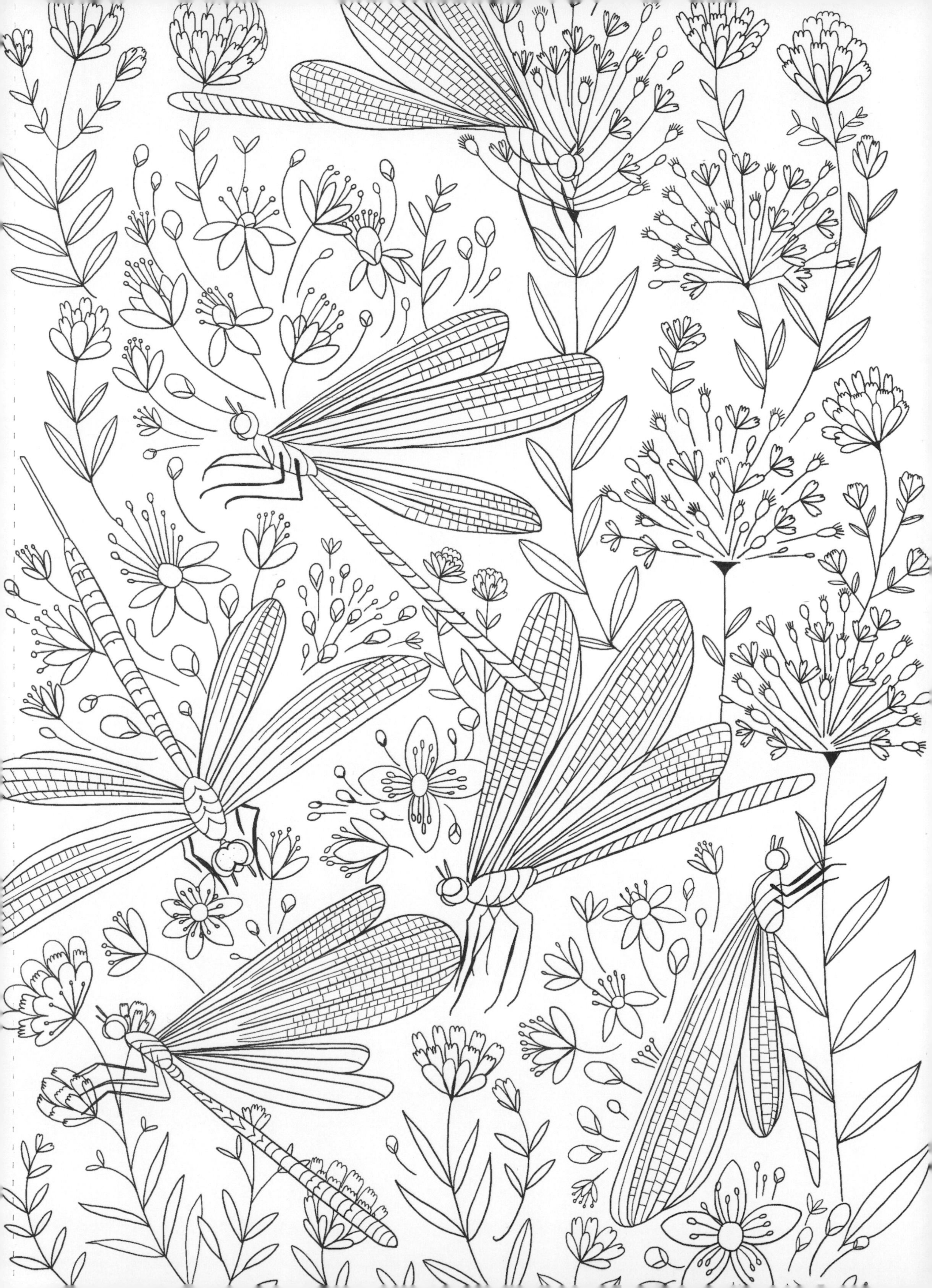

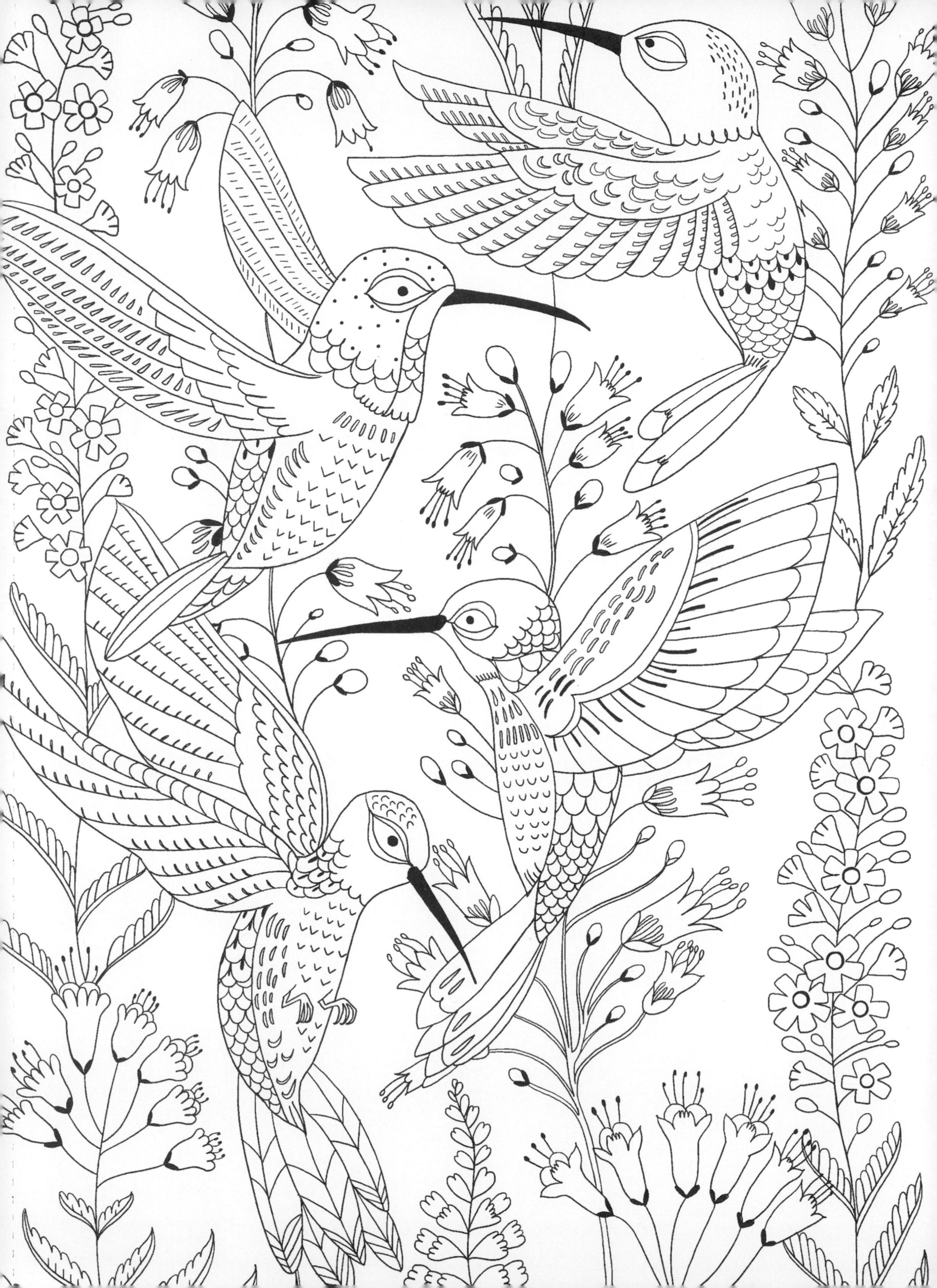

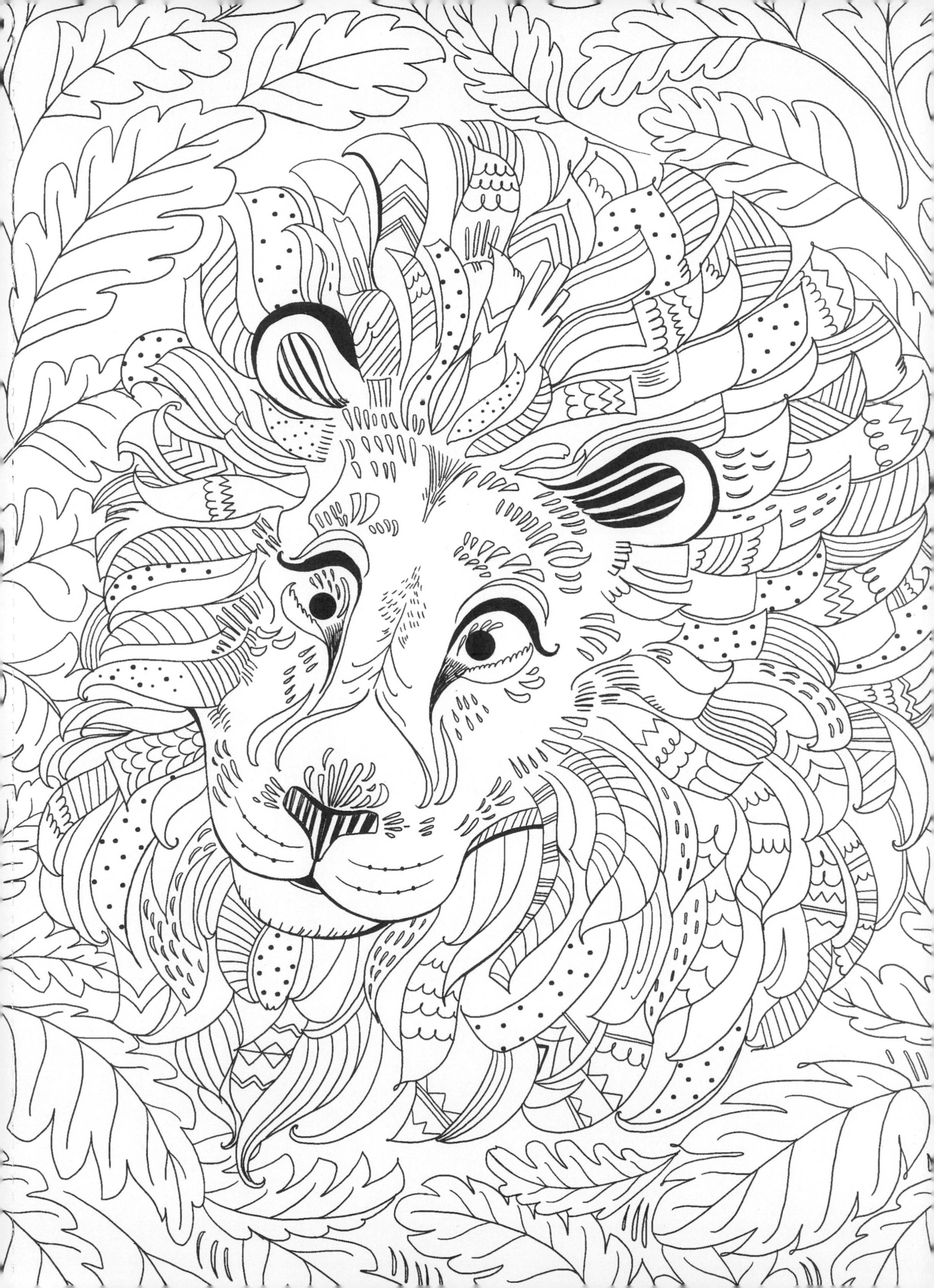

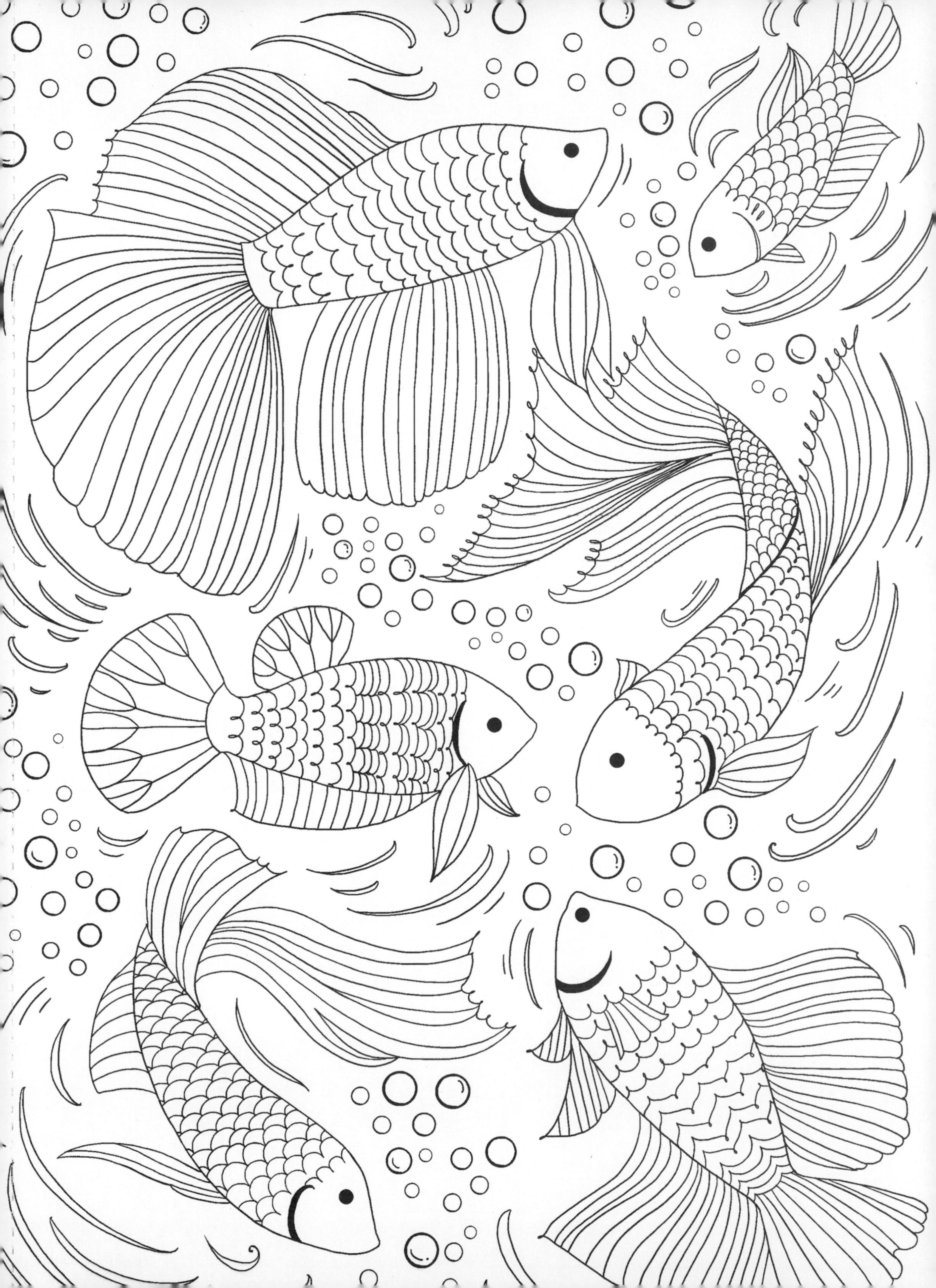

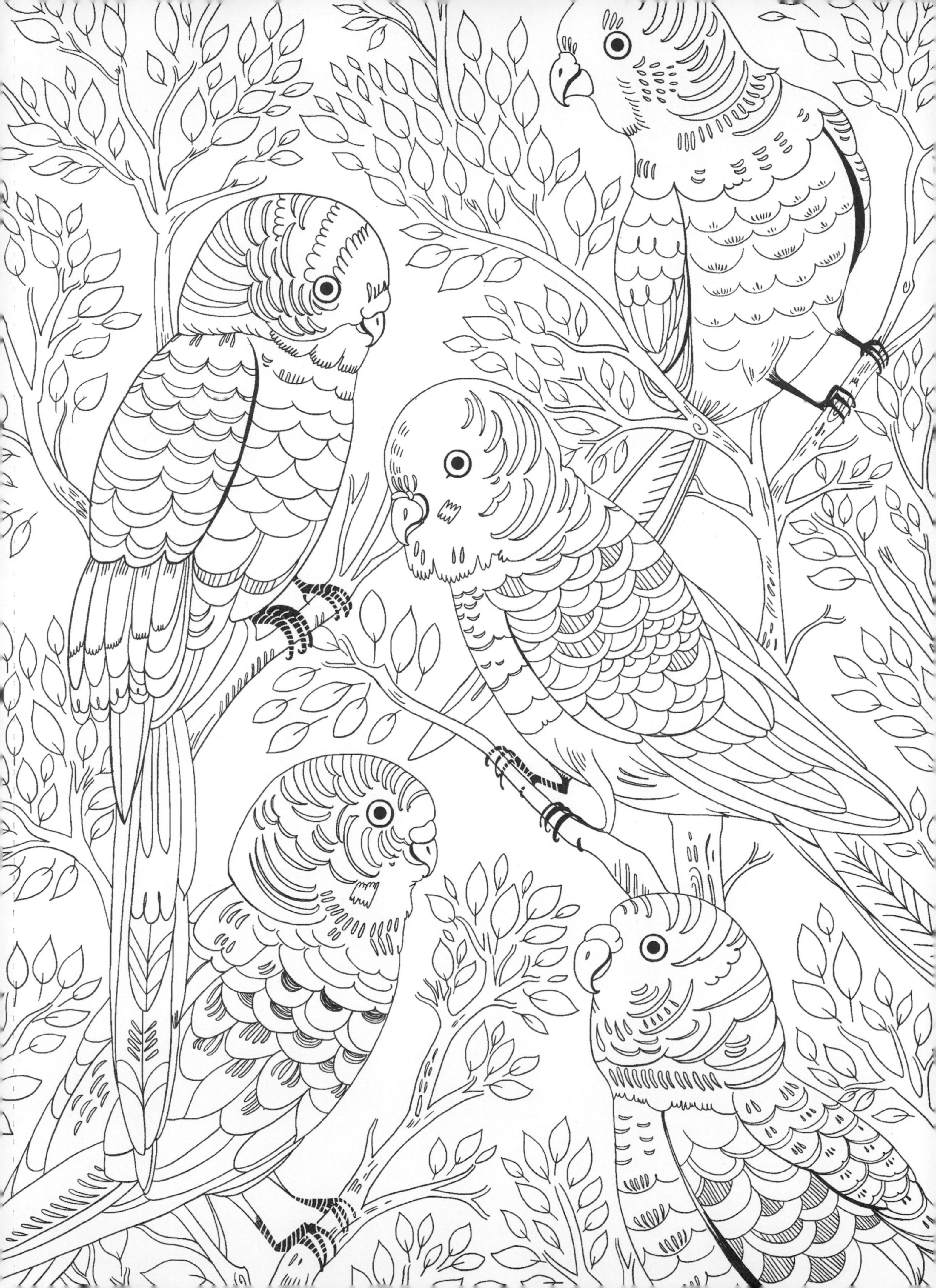

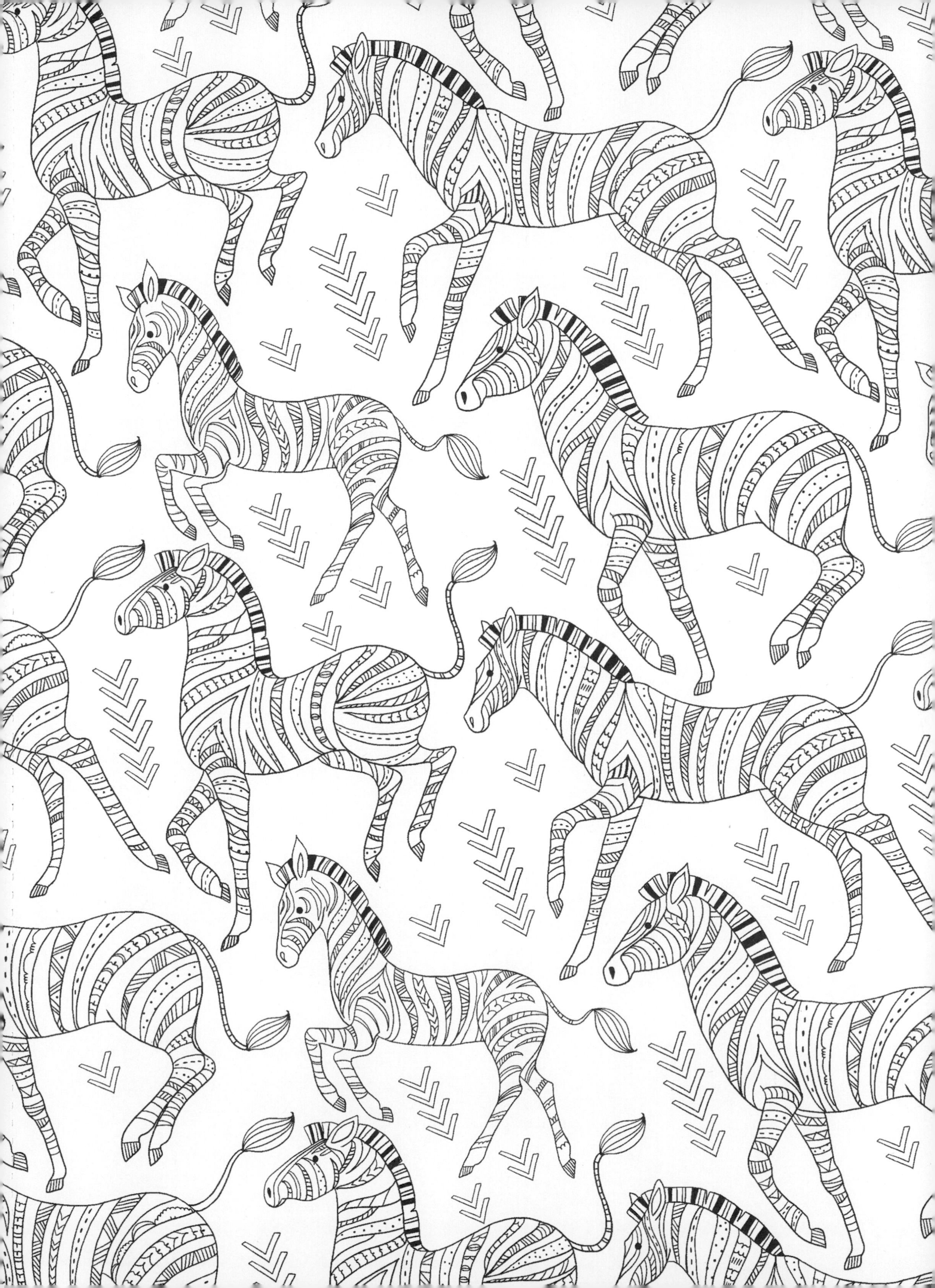

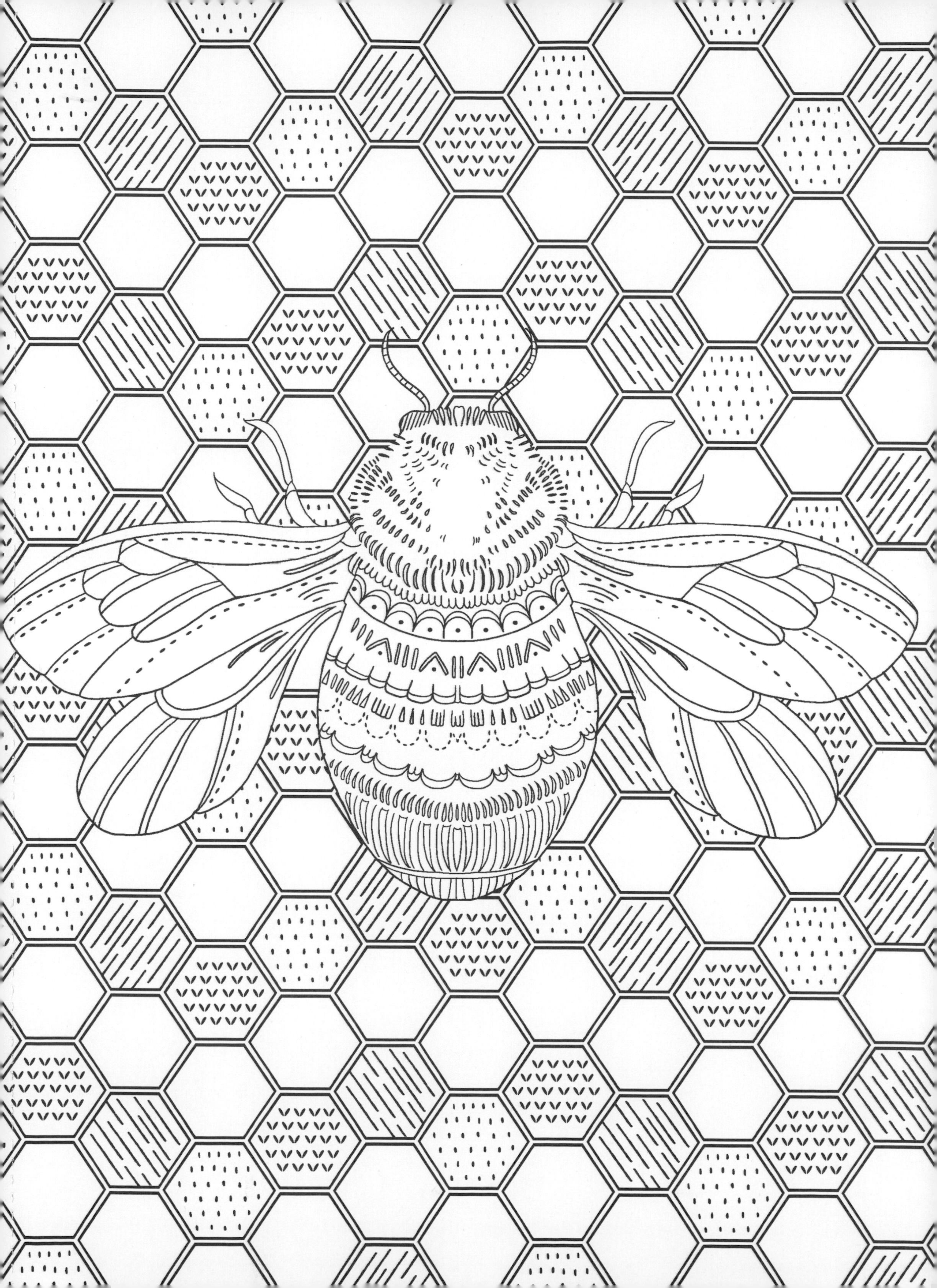

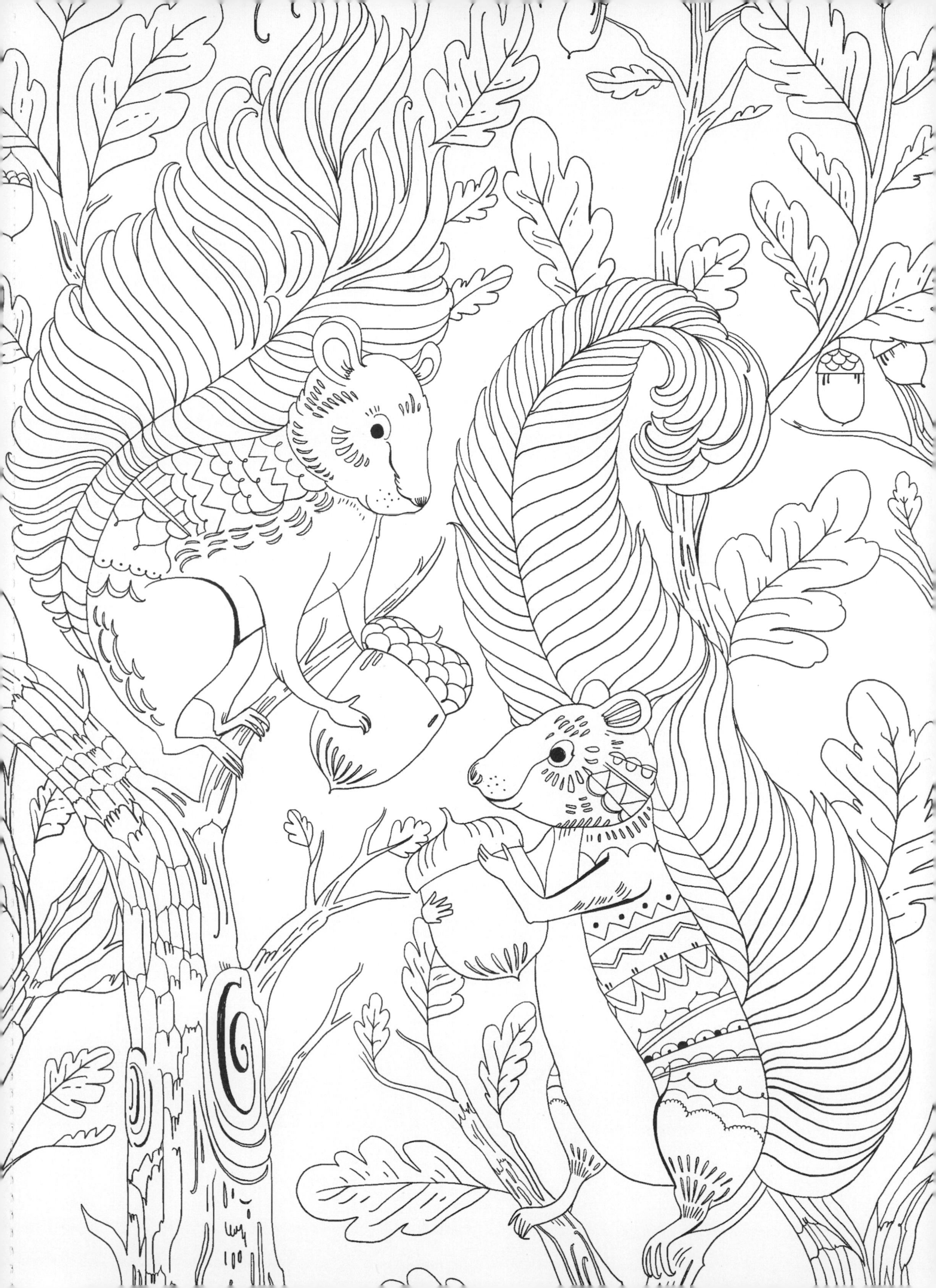

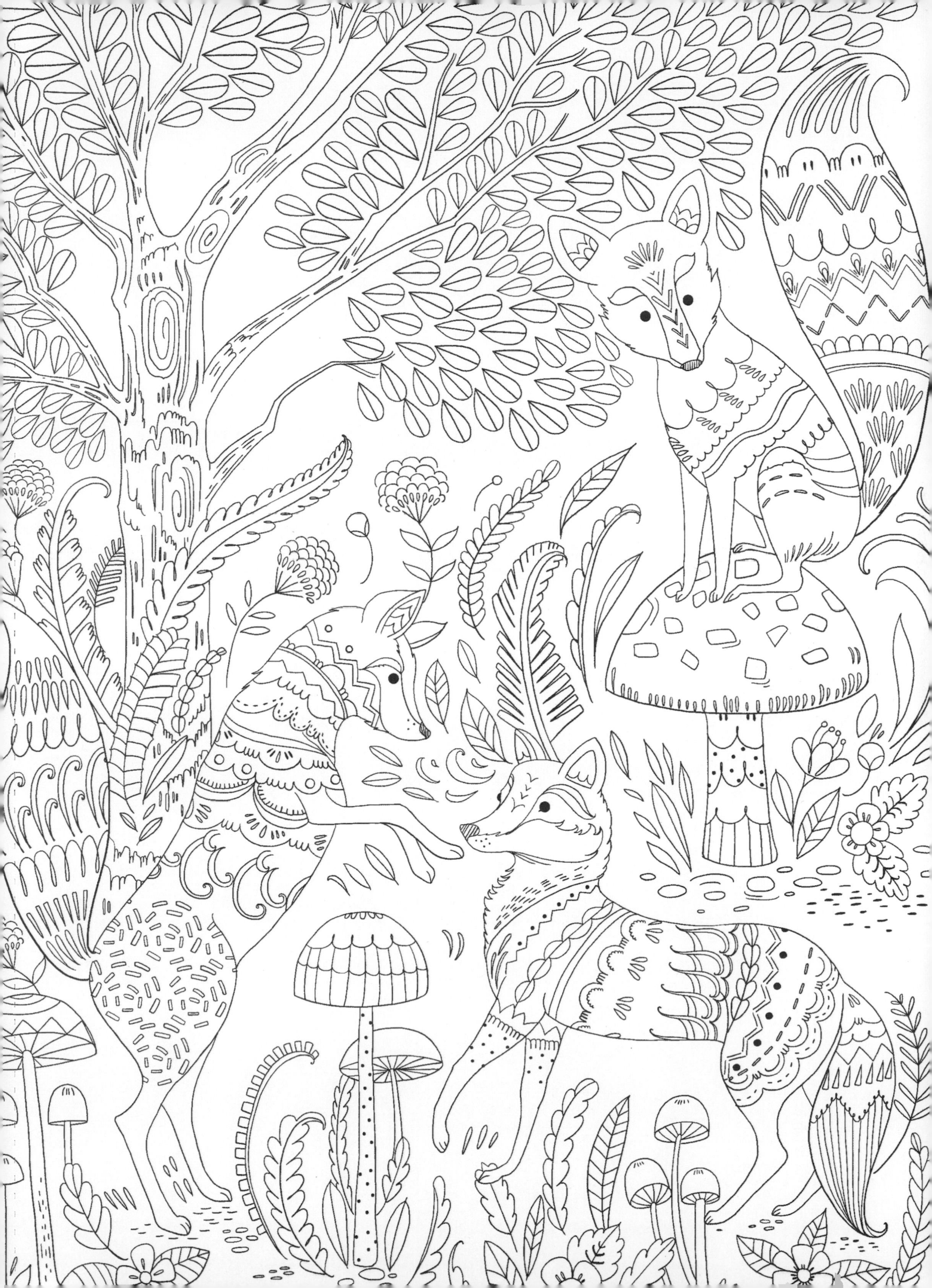

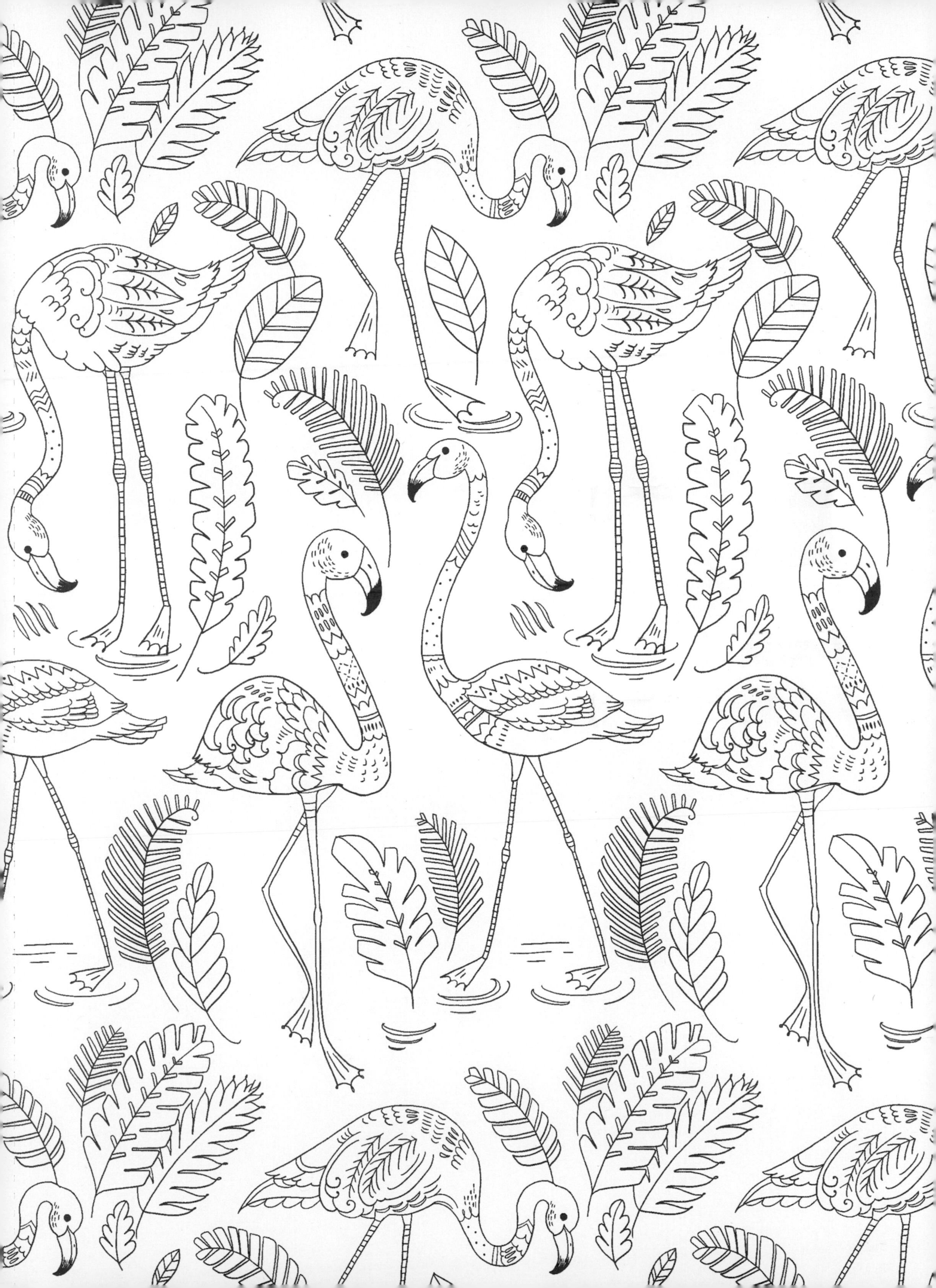

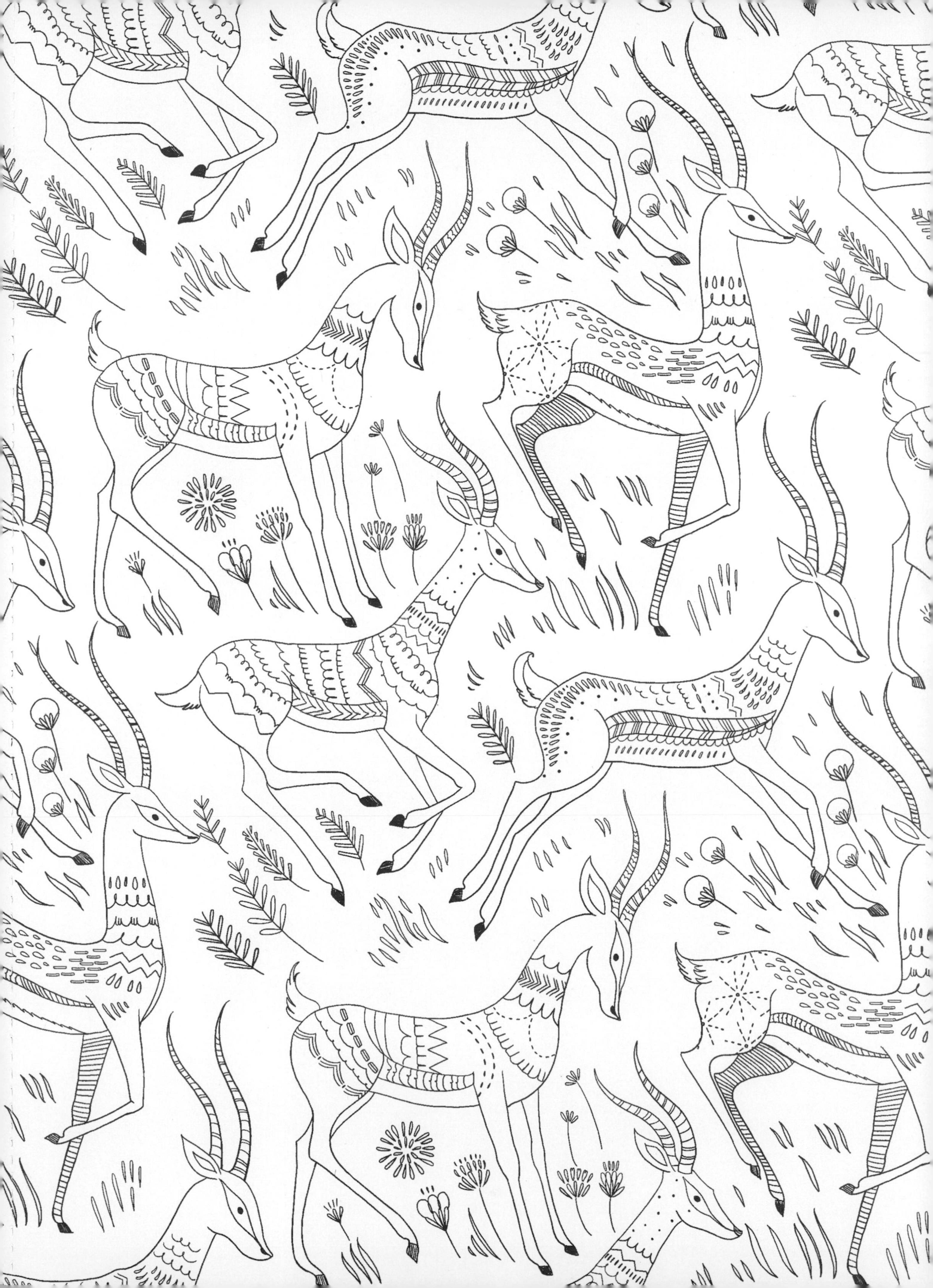

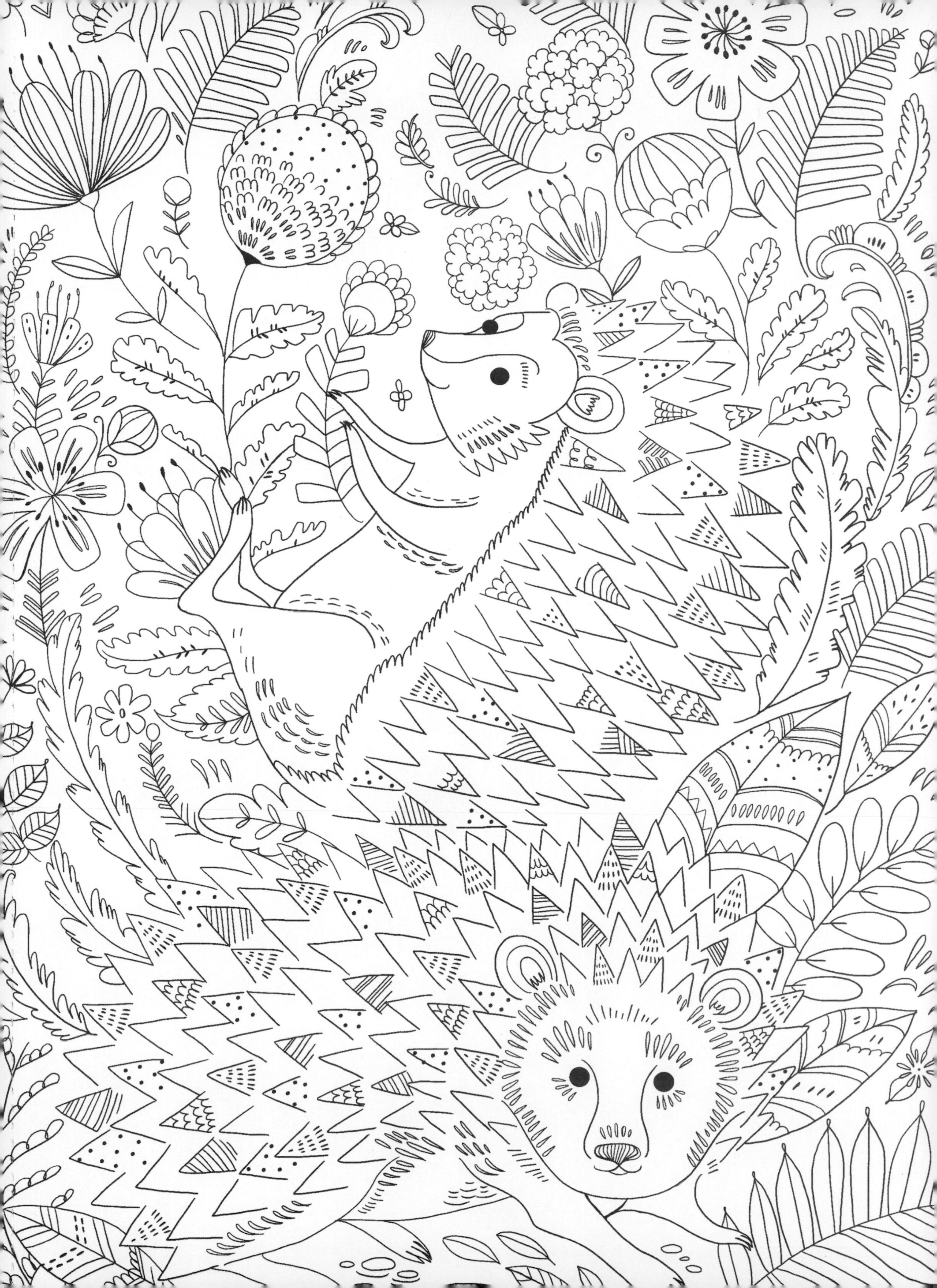

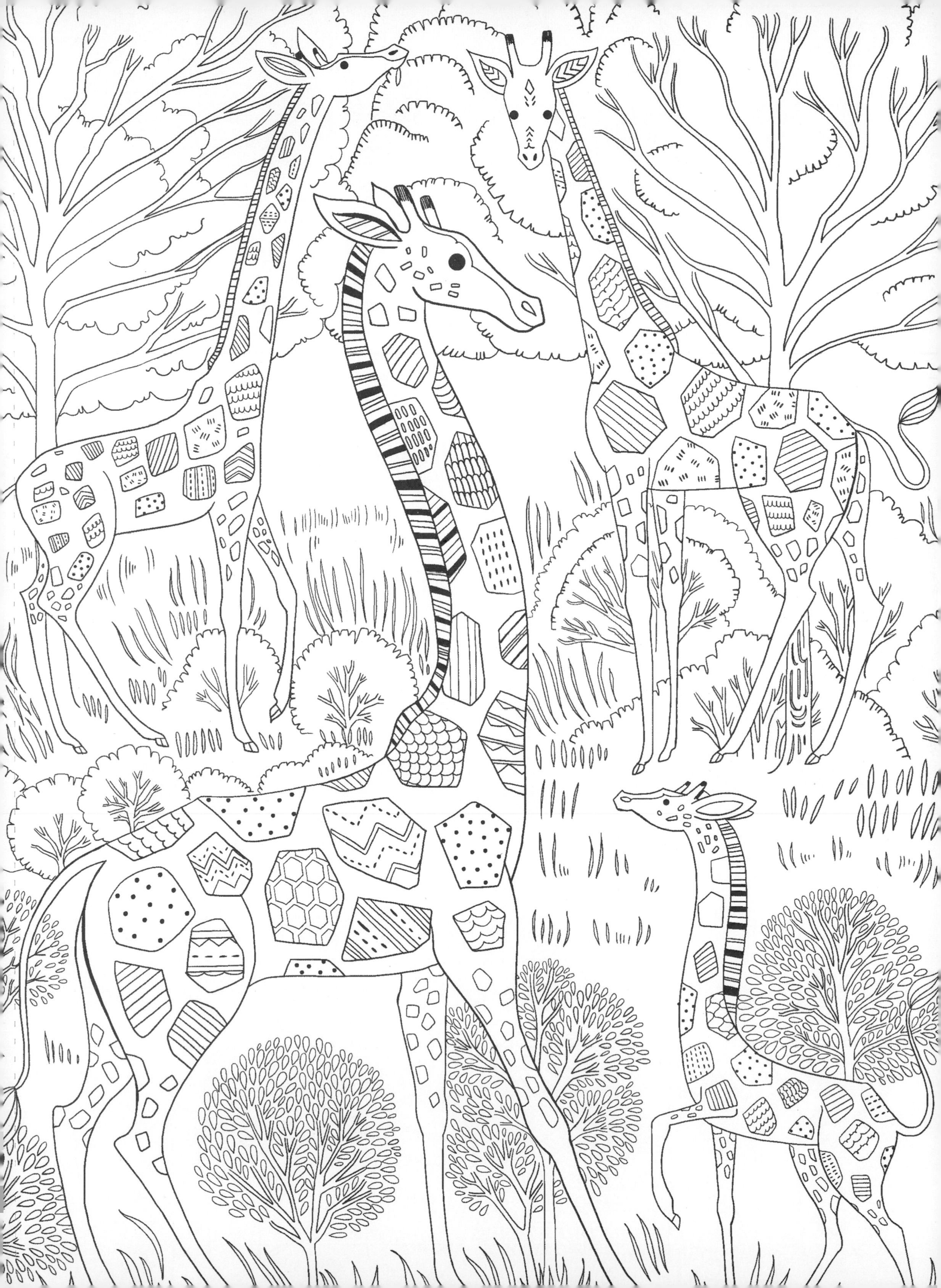

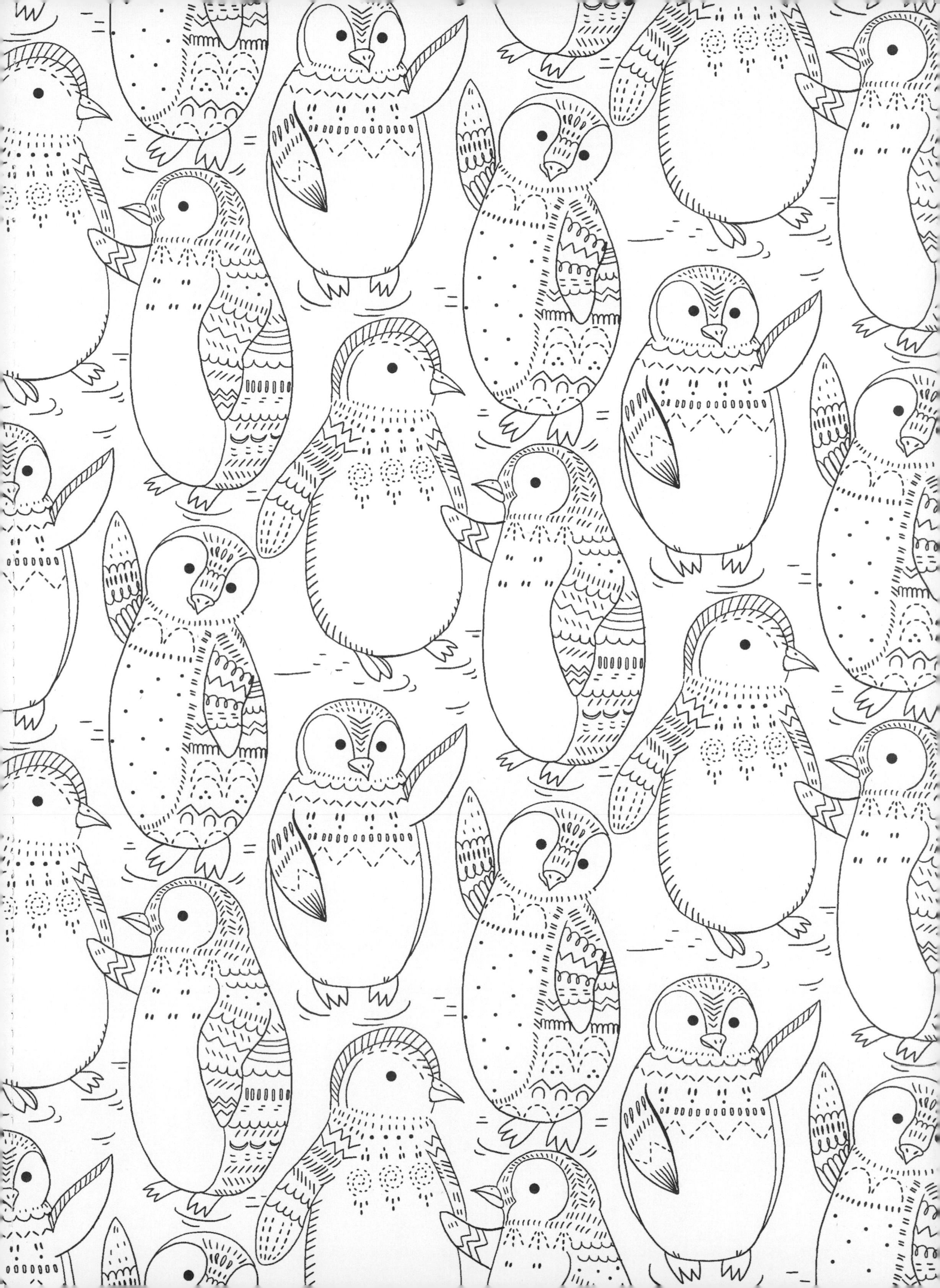

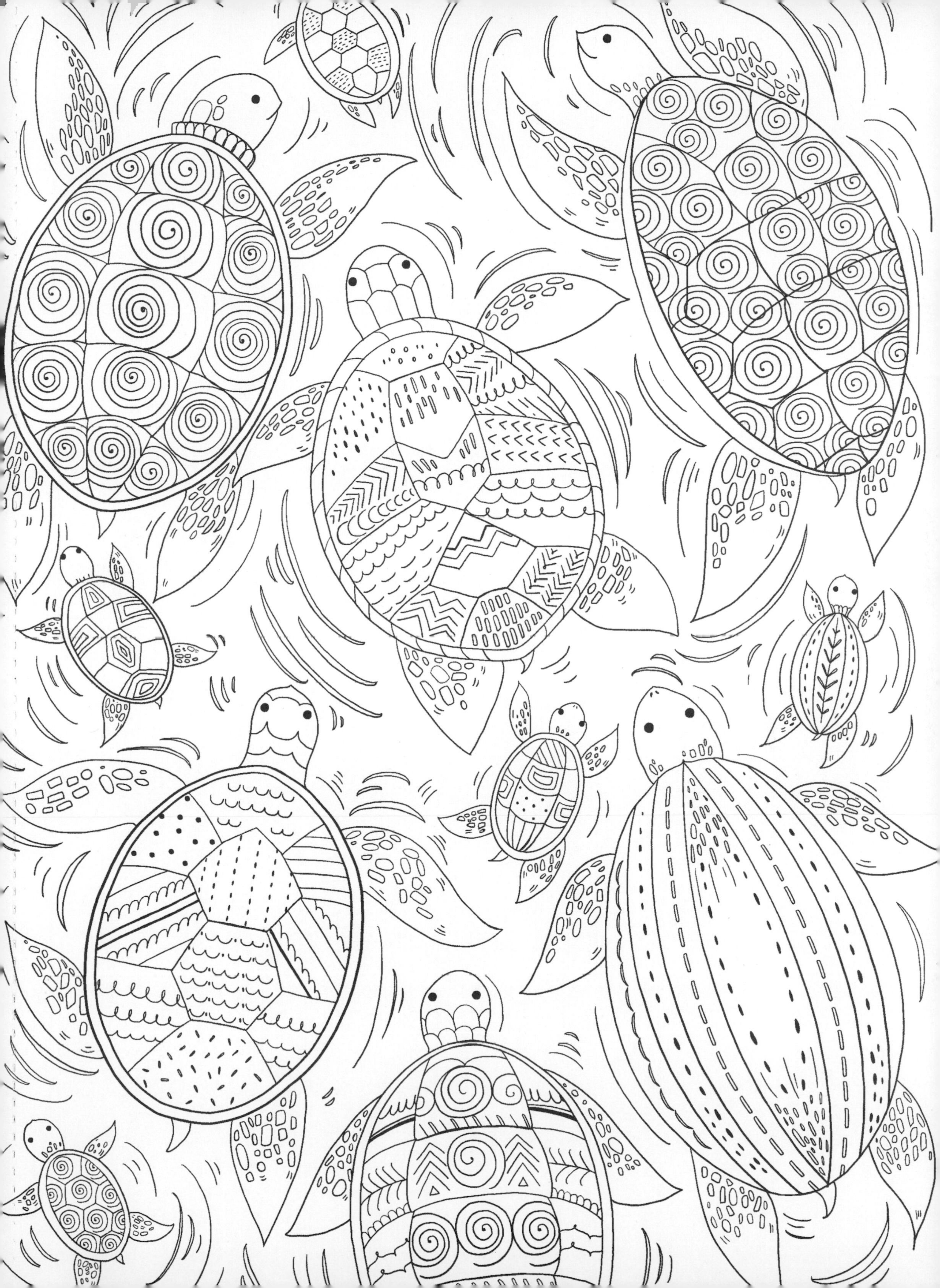

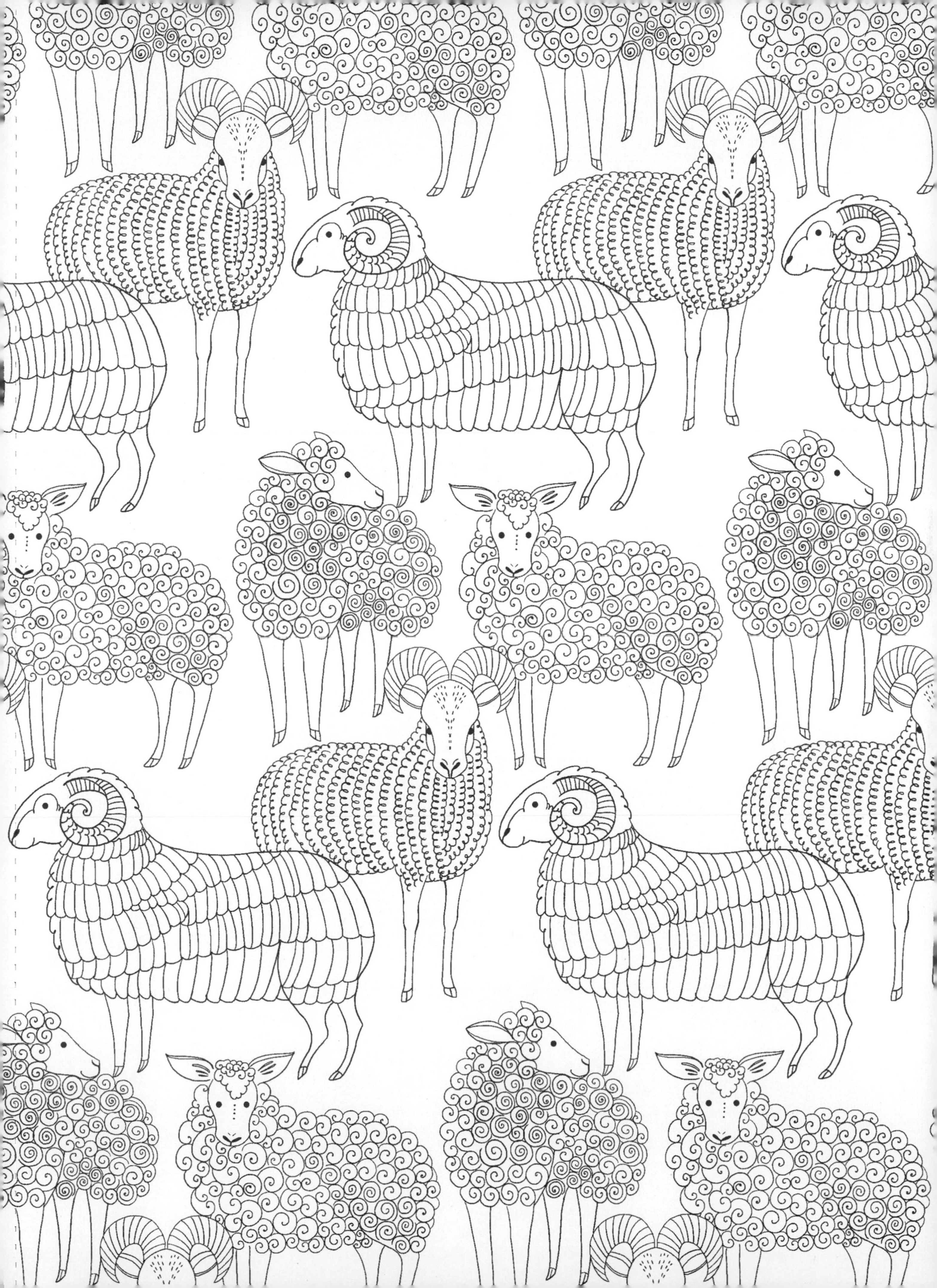

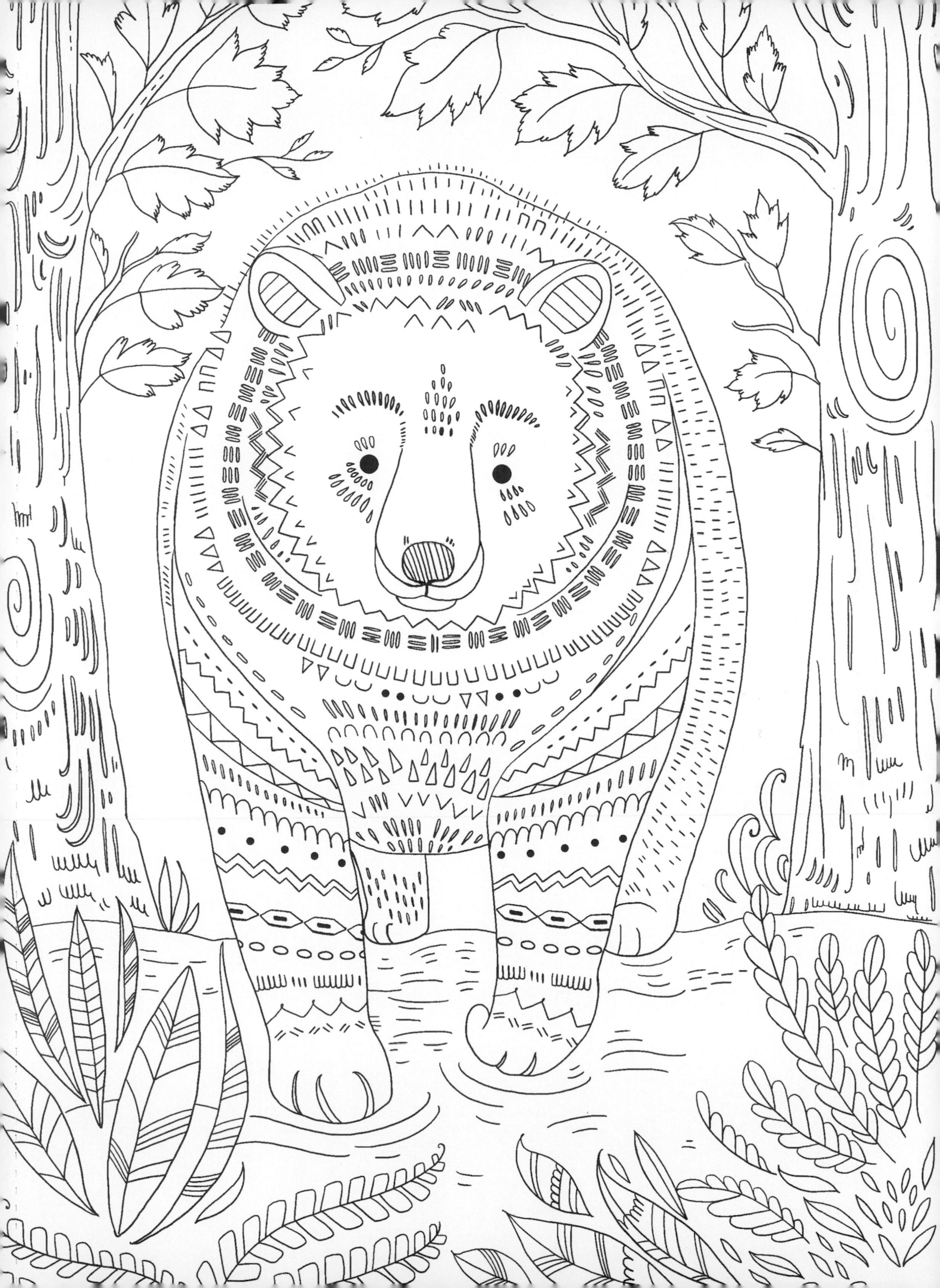

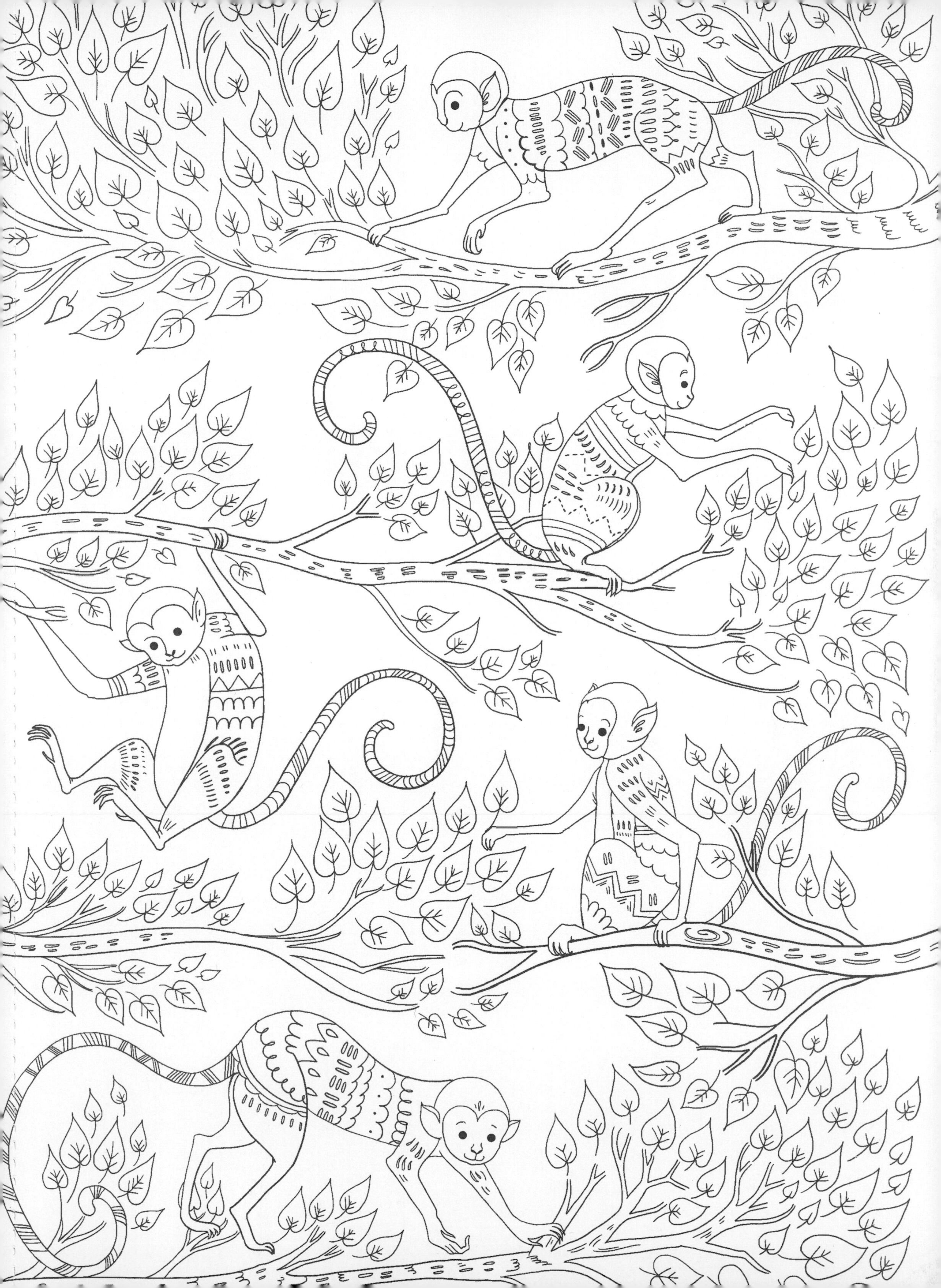

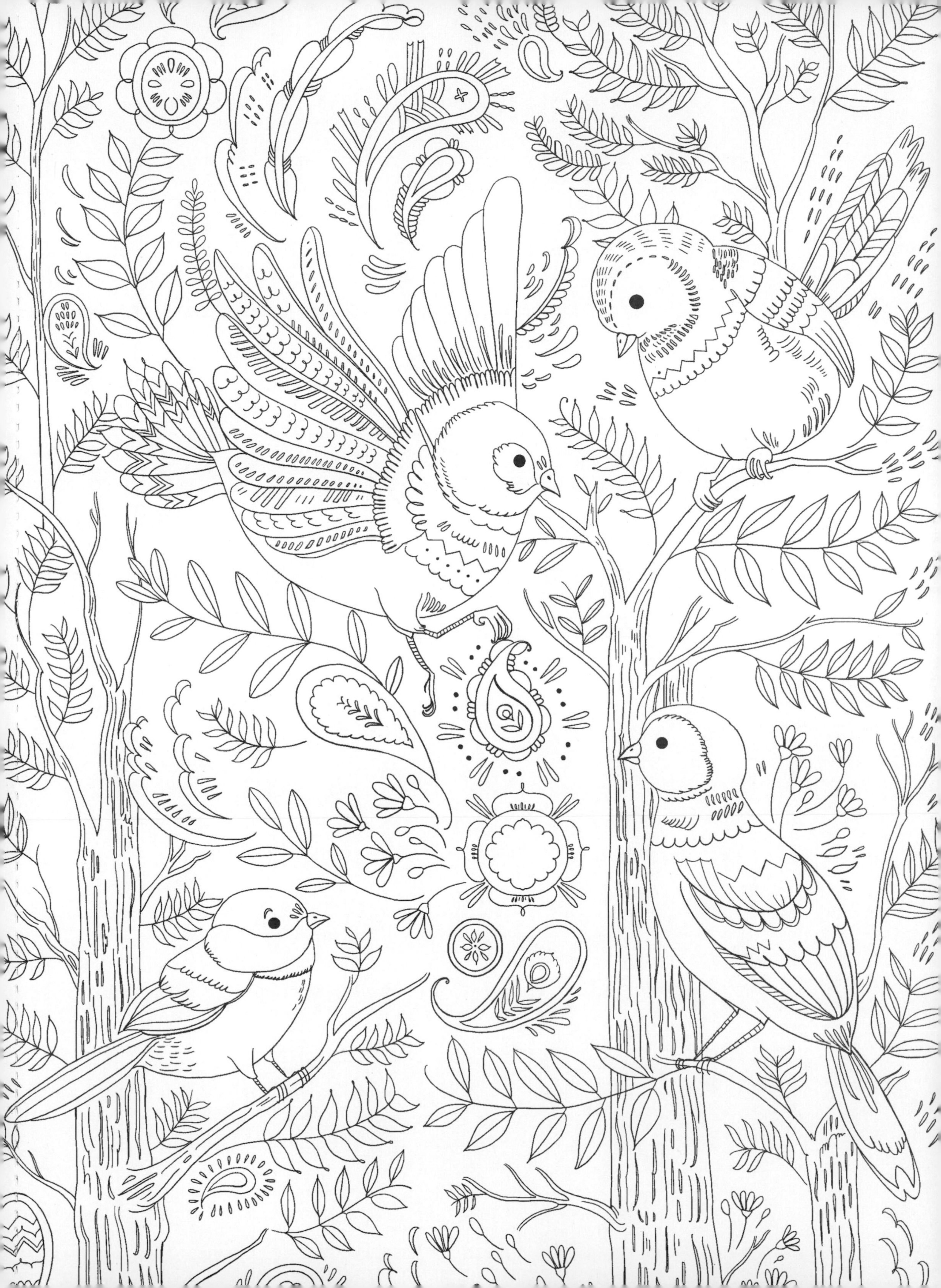

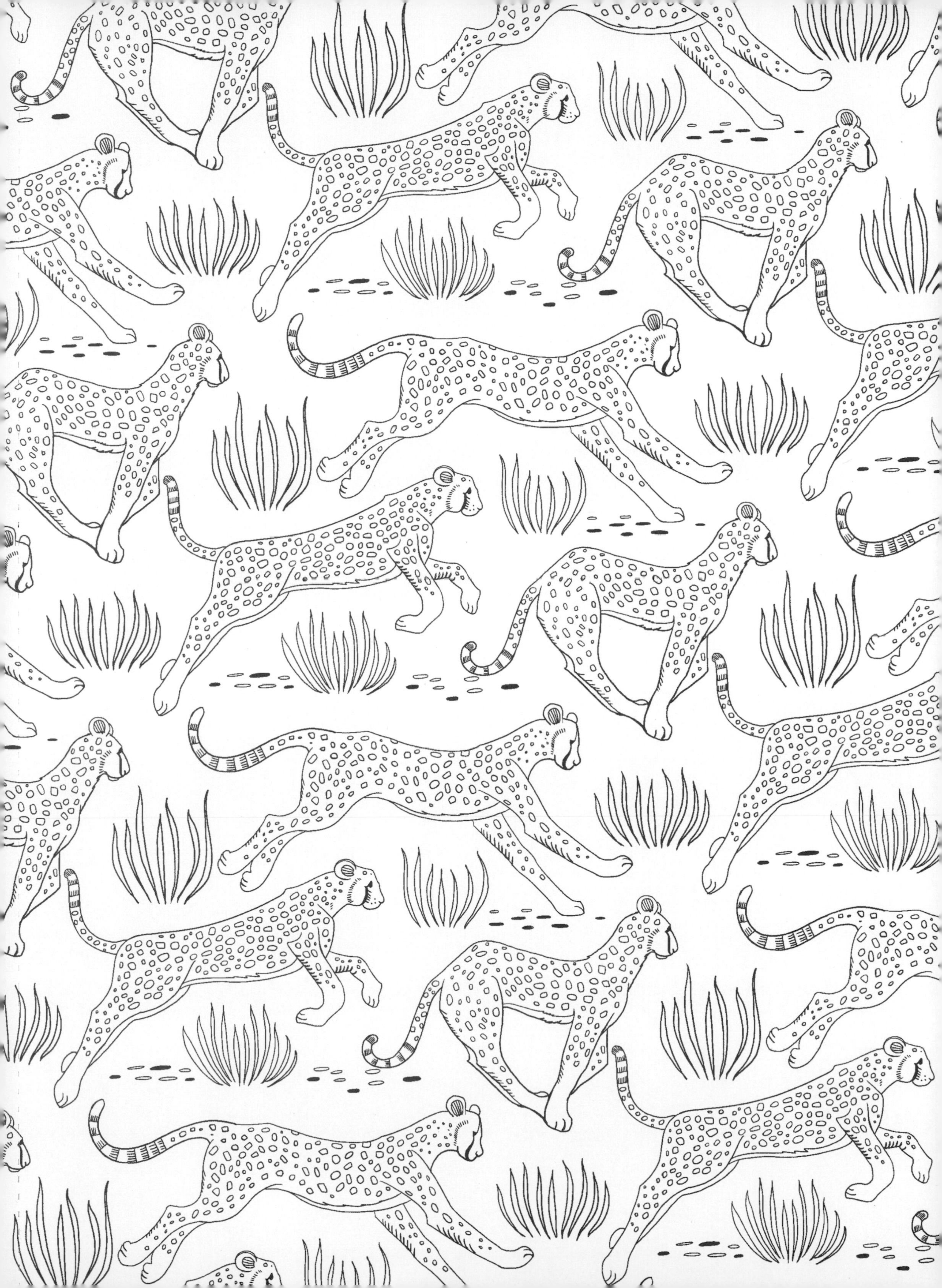

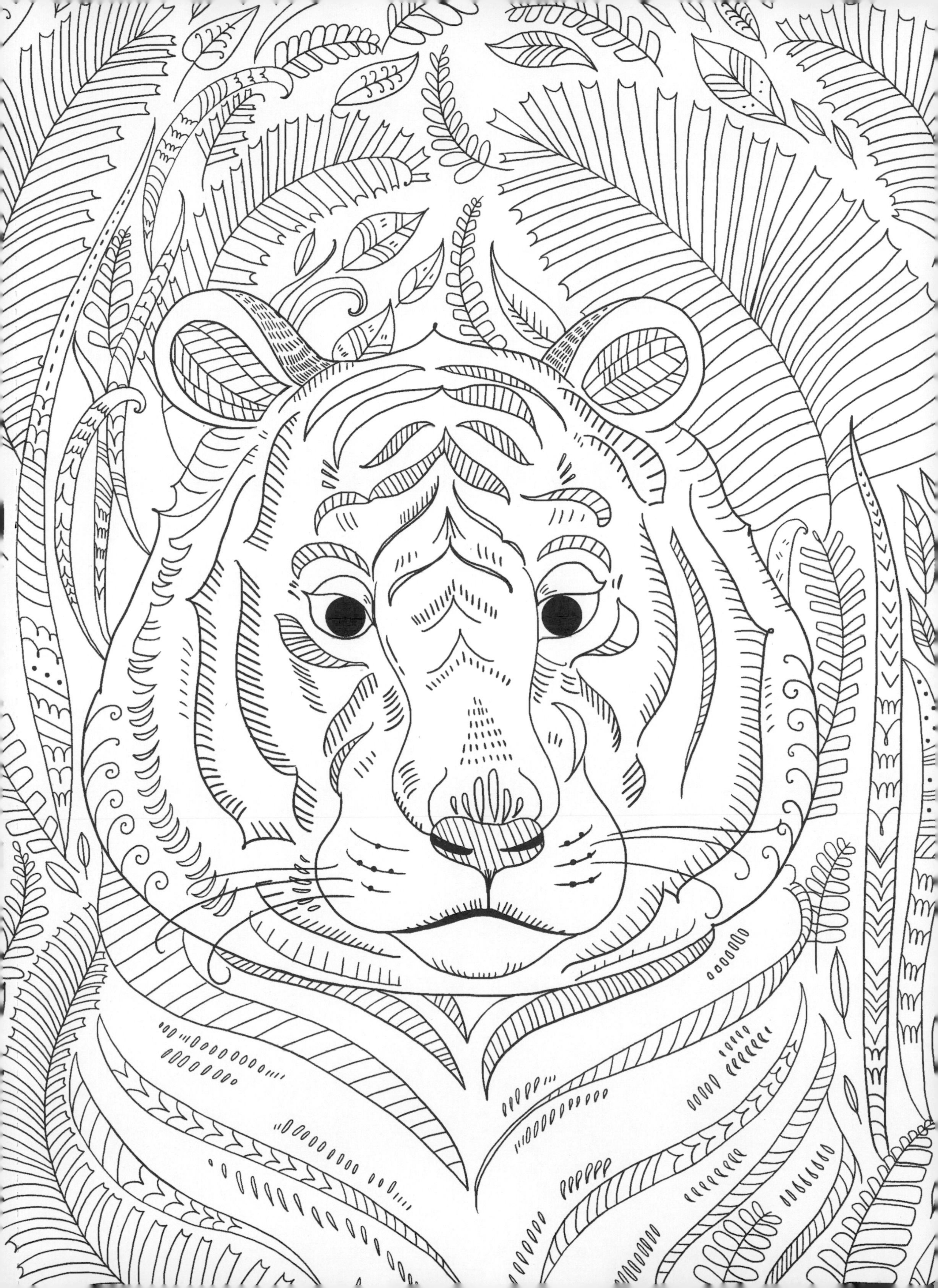